PICTURE FRAMING

PICTURE FRAMING

ROBERT CUNNING

WARD LOCK

First published in Great Britain in 1986
by Ward Lock, Villiers House, 41/47 Strand, London WC2N 5JE

First paperback edition 1990.

A Cassell imprint.

Designed by Niki fforde
Drawings by John Castle

Text filmset in Bodoni
by Tradespools Limited, Frome, Somerset
Printed and bound in Spain by
Graficas Reunidas

ACKNOWLEDGMENTS

My thanks to Jane Wisner for her painstaking and thorough research
into the history of framemaking at many art galleries and libraries,
and for her efforts in typing and correcting the manuscript.

Also my gratitude to Des McNamara for his generosity and guidance.

Special thanks to Maria Zulawski for the loan of her painting by
Marek Zulawski and the frame, and also to Sue Gladstone for the
loan of her three-dimensional frame.

The photographs on pages 11 and 17 were reproduced by the kind
permission of the Tate Gallery, London and City of Bristol Museum
and Art Gallery respectively. All other photographs in the book were
taken by Steve Tanner.

The publishers would like to thank Alex and Shirley Baranowski of
The Framing Shop, 33 Crawford Street, London W1, for the loan of
the framed pictures reproduced on the front jacket cover, including
the oil painting by Michael J. Warren.

British Library Cataloguing in Publication Data

Cunning, Robert
Picture framing.
1. Picture frames and framing—Amateurs'
manuals
I. Title
749'.7   N8550

ISBN 0–7063–6913–0

CONTENTS

INTRODUCTION

Picture framing is often thought of as something that should be left to professionals, and for certain types of frames this is true. However, more and more people are becoming interested in craft work, and picture framing is an ideal pursuit for an enthusiastic beginner. If you are willing to master some simple techniques, and invest a small amount of money in a few basic tools, then a great variety of frames can be made at home, for a comparatively low cost. It is both rewarding and instructive to choose your own picture-frame moulding, cut and assemble a frame, and then decorate it to your own taste.

This book aims to provide the reader with a brief history of the frame and its function in the past; some examples of simple frames that a beginner might try; an inventory of tools that are necessary for the task; instruction in the basic skills of cutting and assembling the parts, including mount cutting; and some advice about the different finishes that can be applied to decorate the completed frame. It should provide the keen beginner with a guide for the pitfalls that are bound to occur in acquiring a new skill. However, only practice will improve the cuts and joinery, as well as the decorative techniques.

The collection of beautiful and interesting objects and works of art is a habit that enriches homes and lives all over the world. Collectors might keep their findings in cupboards and bring them out from time to time, or hide them in bank vaults—but most of us enjoy displaying what we have created or found so that we can live in their presence and share them with others. Thus, the principal reason for a frame's existence is to display pictures and objects, so that we may live with them from day to day and make them part of our surroundings. But why should a frame be necessary?

There are practical as well as aesthetic reasons for framing. The frame provides a hanging support for a picture or object as well as protecting it. For this reason, a good frame must be well constructed and finely finished so that it will stand the test of time and protect as well as enhance the picture or object. Wood or metal surrounds guard the edges and surfaces of paintings. Glass, contained in a frame, protects works on paper and fabric from household conditions of heat, smoke and dust.

A frame must complement a picture, not overpower it; it should not intrude between the viewer and the picture. For example, brightly coloured mounts and ornate frames may sometimes be appropriate, but should not dominate the visual impact of the picture or object. Different subjects require different frames and settings; there are no fixed rules. In general, more traditional frames will suit more traditional styles of painting or decorative work. Modern work, whether photographic, painting, print or reproduction, may be more appropriate in a more minimal presentation, using modern materials. However, 'modern master' paintings are frequently displayed in ornate, gilded, antique period frames—and, conversely, older styles of painting are presented in a more modern manner.

Frames have been used in the West since the Middle Ages, when pictures became a part of church decoration, framed in the architecture of the church. The frame was part of the picture, often fashioned from the same piece of wood that the picture was painted on and sometimes carved and decorated in the same manner as the surrounding architecture. The frame was part of the picture, and part of the architecture; it contained the picture and isolated it from its surroundings, and it related the picture to them. To understand design in relation to frames, observation of successful frames from the past will develop your eye and feed your imagination. Most of the examples in this book are drawn from the present day, but many of them hark back to the past for their inspiration. Pictures in their original frames are rarer than they should be, but these are so well worth viewing that a number of notable ones in national collections have been listed on pages 75–78.

1   A HISTORY OF FRAMES

Both pictures and frames are steeped in the atmosphere of the time and place they were made. The form of frames not only changed in accordance with the style of painting but was linked to the form and decoration of furniture and architecture (inside and out), to social values, whims of fashion, relative prosperity, the identity of individual patrons of the arts, historical events, and to whoever was actually involved in designing or making the frames.

Frames were once designed by architects and artists and carved by fine craftsmen. Some pictures survive with their original frames, but sadly not that many. Although the frame would have been made for the picture, integrated with it and regarded as part of it—the boundary and containing form—it has been considered necessary through the centuries to change the frame to suit the surrounding architectural fashion. If frames had been regarded simply as part of the picture itself (which, after all, is not going to change to suit the fashion of the time), then more would have survived. The Rijksmuseum in Amsterdam is one haven where most of the original Dutch frames have survived.

In the Middle Ages, a picture was sometimes continued over part of the frame, but always the frame fulfilled the function of a border—the kind of border that had already been used by monks in their manuscript pictures to isolate them from the text and to integrate them in the design of the page and lettering. Sometimes the frame was continued into the picture, the artist painting a framework maybe of architectural elements, or a border of figures: saints or angels.

The first free-standing frames are to be found in the later Middle Ages in thirteenth-century European churches and cathedrals. They were designed and made by the same craftsmen who worked on the screens, pulpits and choir-stalls. They framed altar-pieces and small religious works, and were fashioned from the same piece of wood that the picture was painted on. As time progressed, frames became grander and larger, burnished with gold leaf, with more panels often hinged together, and often they stood on a base (known as the predella) which might contain its own small pictures. The frames in time came to be made of extra pieces of wood attached to the panels, which gave better support and guarded against the danger of warps and cracks in the panels.

The small panel paintings of Northern Europe continued to be at one with their frames, the picture area carved out lower than the border. By the fifteenth century portraits were much in evidence, as well as small devotional paintings—and they appeared in private houses. We are given a detailed representation of an artist at work in an early sixteenth-century wing of an altar-piece by the Followers of Quentin Massys (*St Luke Painting the Virgin*, now in the National Gallery, London). The framed panel is propped on an easel and

St Luke the artist holds palette and brushes in his left hand. How little this has changed. He would have coated both panel and frame with a thick smooth white layer of gesso made from animal glue mixed with calcium carbonate (the Italians used calcium sulphate), and then painted them with tempera colours and probably used areas of gilding as well. A simple English example is the portrait of Henry VII in the National Portrait Gallery, London. Even with separate frames, the frame would be joined to the picture panel before the gesso was laid on them both and the frame and painting considered as one integral unit.

In portraits, it became the custom among artists to include details of the subject in writing. If you look at English or German portraits of the period you will often find the date and the age of the subject painted on the plain background either side of the head. Flemish painters supplied this information around the frame, and often on religious paintings they would paint delicate patterns. So that although the shape and moulding of these small frames were comparatively plain, and very similar to how we think of framing today, they were beautifully and painstakingly ornamented, probably by the artists themselves, as part of their picture.

A rare example still exists of an early fifteenth-century French picture where the ornament is carved out of the wood (*Madonna and Child*, in the Frick Collection, New York): a flowing pattern of foliage in quite high relief against a hollowed out border.

The Flemish artists also began to think of the frame as a window on the world of their painting. They painted the border to look like the marble, wood or stone round a window; they used *trompe l'oeil* effects to make the subject appear to be partly in front of the frame; and they sometimes painted a sill at the bottom edge for a hand or sleeve to rest on.

In Italy, great changes were taking place, with the flowering of the Renaissance. The wealthy merchants and nobles added their patronage to that of the Church, and demand grew for a much wider subject matter than portraits or devotional images as artists were called upon in the decorating of palaces and luxurious homes.

Artists became great admirers of the art of ancient Greece and Rome, and began to emulate it and then to experiment with creating the illusion of three-dimensional form and distance in their paintings. Frames, still regarded as part of the picture, had much care and imagination lavished upon them and many innovations were made, in the spirit of the time. Gradually the frames became separate entities designed for individual pictures; artist, patron and carver collaborated in their design and execution.

Circular paintings (roundels or tondos) became quite common, instigated by masters like Botticelli and inspired by Luca della Robbia, who in Tuscany made terracotta medallions surrounded by moulded wreaths of flowers and leaves. Michelangelo's *The Holy Family* (in the Uffizi Gallery, Florence), painted in 1504, has a frame carved by Antonio Basile of Siena which gives us an idea of just how far these Renaissance personalities stretched their imagination and skills to develop an idea. It presents us too with a perfect example of how an exceptionally detailed and ornate frame, through its tone, its proportion and the placing of detail, can greatly enhance a painting rather than detract from it. The contrast between painting and frame serves to emphasize the clarity and intensity of this great picture, and the placing of detail is in direct relationship to its composition. In an era when architecture, painting, sculpture and all the crafts were so closely interconnected (painters often excelled in sculpture and architecture and other crafts), it is not surprising that such a harmony between picture and frame was achieved in this manner.

Another type of frame that developed was inspired by

Old Battersea Bridge *by James McNeill Whistler. Whistler designed the frames for all his paintings, and this reeded frame is characteristic of his work. The artist's distinctive butterfly marking can be seen on the right-hand side of the frame.*

ancient Greek architecture, and both altar-pieces and small devotional paintings are found with the quiet classical proportions, pilasters and cornices. Later frames in the same vein retained the proportions but omitted the architectural elements, the picture simply being surrounded by a flat painted inner moulding. Some paintings were set into the wall, and their frames tended to be even simpler.

The frame that evolved was the 'border' frame, and this was completely free from architectural elements and so concentrated more on the picture it framed. It had three bands of ornamentation, combined in beautiful calm proportions; each band was highly ornamented but the detail was subservient to the outline and the pattern was quite formal, derived from ancient architectural detail. Raised narrow inner and outer mouldings would be reeded or plain, burnished with gold; the wider middle panel set lower between the two mouldings, and usually flat, might be painted or embossed with delicate floral patterns. The combination of pattern and proportion varied greatly but the effect was one of subtlety: subdued, very delicate detail—and even the brightness of the gilding was toned down by the application of a thin transparent glue mixed with a dash of pigment. These frames have much to say to the frame-maker of today, who will be playing with precisely the same elements in a simple modern frame: the relationship of proportion and details of picture and frame. In Chapter 2 there is a description of the techniques for making such a frame.

So these were the frames of the High Renaissance. As time progressed Italian frames became more and more elaborately carved, and although the picture might be contained in a linear moulding, the carving of the wide border and outer mouldings became loose, flowing, heavier and more ornate until they were no longer delineated. The calm, quiet proportions of the earlier frames were superseded.

The influence of Italy during its Renaissance spread far and wide, and each European country adopted the ideas generated in Florence, Siena and Venice, and developed them in their own character. Germany concentrated on carving dense, crisp decoration often ornamented with ivory inlays, shells, copper and semi-precious stones. Spain adopted a stronger, simpler, heavier ornamentation with a feeling for the wood that was being carved, and used a very dark tone for its gold leaf.

In England, the reign of Henry VIII (1509–1547) brought many foreign craftsmen and demand grew for paintings and frames, both for the great palace collections of the king and in private homes. After the suppression of the monasteries, craftsmen went into secular service and found a market for their skills in private homes. The inventories for Henry VIII's palaces in 1542 list pictures painted on canvasses as well as panels, in tempera or oil, and these paintings would have been framed in wood with gold or silver, and possessed shutters or silk curtains for protection. Carving at this time was Renaissance in character but still with a trace of the Gothic. The Tudors liked to decorate woodwork with painted graining or marbling as well as gilding—and picture frames were no exception. Henry VIII's portrait in the National Portrait Gallery, London (1520), has a painted grained frame.

In the sixteenth and seventeenth centuries the focus of the arts was shifting from Italy to France, where François I (1515–1547) invited many Italian craftsmen and artists to court. Not only the royal palaces became lavishly furnished and decorated, but also the increasingly prosperous middle-class homes. Frames, instead of being designed and made by artists and sculptors, became the province of the furniture designers, and were regarded as part of interior decoration.

Louis XIV institutionalized sculpture and painting, and

picture frames (and mirror frames), vigorously carved and ornamental, were designed by eminent artists and made on a grand scale by highly organized guilds of cabinet-makers. Consequently, the types of frame were standardized compared to the variety and individuality of those from the different regions of Italy in previous years. Louis XIII frames took their inspiration from certain Bolognese and Venetian ones, using oak leaves or vine leaves and flowers in shallow carving over a convex shape, with no projections outward or forward. Louis XIV frames had the accent on corners and the centre of each edge, which projected over the outside of the frame. Their entire surface was gilded; they would have needed to be lavish in order to compete with the surrounding opulence of the period. *Régence* frames, which followed, still had the carved corners and centres but they were linked by plain panels bordered by straight edges.

French frames became admired for their clearly defined ornament, made possible by a technique known as re-cutting. The whole frame would be carved in oak, covered in its coats of gesso, and then the decoration would be recarved in detail and the background cross-hatched. This work would be done by a specialist craftsman called a *repareur*. These frames became popular all over Europe, especially in England and the Netherlands, as French craft was recognized.

In spite of the spreading influence of the French, seventeenth-century Dutch frames enjoyed their own most individual development, although their original inspiration had also been the Italian Renaissance border frame. Dutch craftsmen had great feeling for the qualities of the wood itself. They carved it with restraint, using repetitive motifs around the various bands of the frame, and they often painted it black with very little use of gilding or colouring. These frames matched the quietness and discipline of their paintings. Dutch homes were very different from their French counterparts because, al-though bankers and merchants were prosperous, their Protestant taste was refined and lavish opulence was not appreciated. So the small, quiet, restrained paintings of Vermeer are seen in plain, wide, dark, wooden frames with rippled borders, often with the window further from the wall than the outer edge, presenting the picture out towards the viewer. Dutch merchant shippers began to import ebony and fruit-wood and many other excitements that inspired the frame-makers to use veneers of wood, tortoise-shell and turtle-shell. Cabinet-makers designed and made the frames on a large, organized scale as in France. They employed special machines to cut the patterns into veneers, which were laid on to the surface of the moulded frames in an infinite variety of combinations. They had a fine sense of proportion.

A later desire for more ostentatious frames generated a Dutch version of the carved and gilded frame, known as a Lutma frame after its instigator, the Amsterdam goldsmith Johan Lutma. Originally derived from Venetian frame design, these are wide and flat with their undulating carving very much adhering to their flat background which has little or no moulding to frame the picture. The motifs used are naturalistic flowing forms of, maybe, fruit and flowers, birds, cherub heads or objects connected with the subject of the painting; they overlap the outer edge of the frame with an emphasis on the centre of the top and bottom and sometimes the centre of the sides. The Dutch frame-makers, when they used gold leaf, favoured a duller sheen than that of their French contemporaries; to this end they used not a shiny gesso ground but a base of oil paint, and sometimes a coloured varnish. The gold leaf was used sparingly, perhaps only on some of the raised lines of ornament.

English frames were influenced either by Holland or France, according to shifts in politics and social values. Charles I played a part in supporting and encouraging painting. He formed a large collection of pictures, and guilds of carvers, joiners and gilders were responsible for making frames (the carpenters' guild was not concerned with frame making). They began to create lavish pieces of work. During the Commonwealth, frames were comparatively plain, but after the Restoration in 1660 the reaction was a hankering after luxurious French designs, and frames were carved and decorated lavishly with scrolls or leaf motifs. Charles II demonstrated a love of luxury. He was brought up in France and Holland and had a Portuguese wife. During his reign trade with the Far East increased. All this influenced design, and English craftsmen were considered the equal of their foreign counterparts.

A popular type of frame at this time was known as the *genre auriculaire*, a carved and gilt frame decorated with fairly flat auricular scrolls. There is a pair of these frames in Dulwich Art Gallery, London, made in about 1670, one of them with a portrait of the king. The Long Gallery in Ham House, London, is full of these frames, and well worth a visit. From Vermeer's painting *Gentleman and Lady Drinking* (Berlin) it can be seen that these frames were also used for Dutch pictures of the time, for one hangs on the wall in the background.

During the Restoration, too, it was common to have pictures framed by mouldings incorporated into the usual panelled walls of houses. These mouldings in the wainscoting could be plain or decorated.

At the end of the seventeenth century the influx of the Huguenots in England brought the talent and influence of their carvers, gilders and cabinet-makers from France. At the same time, William and Mary favoured Dutch designs. For the first time one could acquire standard patterns from frame-makers. Oval frames appeared at this time; there was a fashion for oval canvases, and paintings were also made as an oval painted on a rectangular canvas, so that they could be framed in an ordinary rectangular frame.

The Dutch carver, Grinling Gibbons, had a small shop near Ludgate Hill, London. He exhibited a carved pot of flowers in his window 'carved with such delicacy that the leaves shook at the movement of passing coaches'. His frames for both pictures and mirrors were made chiefly in limewood; and the figures, birds, fruit, flowers, ribbons, garlands, tendrils, shells, heads in bold relief, with which he decorated them, were deeply undercut and realistically portrayed, exceedingly detailed and overflowing from the edges of their frames. Gibbons became Master Carver to George I in 1714, and had many fine imitators too.

William Kent (1684–1748) was the first English architect to undertake the complete layout of a house and estate, from ceiling decoration to gardens. He was an exuberant baroque designer, who reacted against the Dutch and French influences. In the Victoria and Albert Museum, London, there is a pinewood mirror frame, carved and gilded, that was made between 1730 and 1740. This was probably designed by William Kent for Frederick Prince of Wales because the same motif was used by Kent on the Prince's barge. The oval mirror frame is very ornate, but organized into a simple design centred on the bearded head at the top with a feathered crown radiating from it, and with hanging flowers at the base of the frame.

Thomas Chippendale, designer and cabinet-maker, also excelled in lavish carving on his frames for mirrors and pictures. He followed a current English interest in Chinese motifs by employing bamboo, rocks, bird cages and Chinese figures in some of his frames. In Paris in the 1720s began the whimsical, decorative, sinuous design of frames in what was called the rococo style, which paid no attention to classical proportion. Chippendale was its main advocate in England. For an example of his art, his frame made for the Prince of Wales's portrait in 1755 can be seen in the Victoria and Albert Museum. Portraits of royal personages were often surmounted by a crown carved over the frame. Later on, military trophies or emblems of the sea, related to the subject of their portrait, were carved in the same position on the frame.

Frame making was a specialist activity contracted by the cabinet-makers to carvers, who made nothing but frames. At this time, there were two kinds of specialist carvers: hardwood carvers and softwood carvers. Those who made frames would be the latter, working in conjunction with the gilders. They would also be the makers of stands, chairs, settees, side-tables and an occasional centre table. In 1733 the duty on imported timber was abolished and mahogany became fashionable; one even can find mahogany frames, but they are not so common.

With centre ornaments and corner embellishments, frames had to be individually carved. But in the early nineteenth century composition was beginning to take the place of carving. Whiting, resin and size were heated and amalgamated, and pressed into moulds of boxwood. The ornament was then applied to a basic wooden profile. The use of plaster or composition when backed with wire meant that detail could protrude from the frame to create delicate ornamentation. Papier maché was also used. Because it is much cheaper and quicker to mould composition than it is to carve wood, the ever-increasing demand for frames meant that its use eventually became the norm.

In France, at the end of the eighteenth century, a more severe style of decoration was in vogue, known as neo-classicism, in reaction to the extravagant taste of rococo. It had begun in Rome. Louis XVI frames were, once again, of plain geometric form with precise detailing on the mouldings of reeded lines, undulating ribbons, foliage, pearls or fluting, in small repetitive patterns with plain flat bands; they were rectangular or oval, and some were surmounted by crowns or wreaths.

Robert and James Adam in England revolutionized English fashion after their visits to Dalmatia and Italy in 1758, where Pompeii and Herculaneum had been discovered. They brought back with them detailed studies of ancient Roman and Greek architecture, and Robert Adam included in his own architecture interior decorations, fittings and furniture with anglicized adaptations of all that the brothers had seen in Italy. His work can be seen in Harewood House in Yorkshire, in Kenwood House (Hampstead Heath), and Syon House, London. He used painted ornament rendered in relief; light, delicate work. Frames echoed the scheme of ornament of whatever was beneath them—mantelpiece or side-table. The accent was on simplicity, lightness and calm lines: a coherent whole. In the library at Osterley Park House, London, which was designed in 1766, the frame over the mantelpiece for a picture by Antonio Zucchi is plain, with ornament outside the geometric shape of the frame. Adam's mirrors were of gilded wood, often oval with projecting husks and hanging festoons held by cupids, and using urns and fanciful vases.

In the Victoria and Albert Museum there is a Georgian pole-screen of carved mahogany from the late eighteenth century, with a very thin frame, which is a beautiful way of framing a delicate watercolour.

At the beginning of the nineteenth century in France, during the reign of Napoleon, came a love of uniformity. The 'Empire' frame often employed plaster motifs derived from palm leaves, lotus and papyrus—discovered in the campaigns in Egypt—as well as the usual classical forms. It was a comparatively plain frame, but with deeply moulded curves. Most paintings in the Louvre in Paris were reframed in this style and the old frames lost; and many museums and private collectors in Europe, unfortunately, followed Napoleon's example.

The nineteenth century saw the first mass-produced frames, all of plaster or composition on a base of wood, which unfortunately has a tendency to crack or flake off after a certain amount of time has gone by. All kinds of frames that had gone before were reproduced in abundance, often with a simulated gold leaf made from brass and bronze powder. In England in Victorian times many rococo imitations were in vogue, until the 1880s when there was a revival of neo-classicism and of Adam's designs. The oval was revived, this time often in the form of a rectangular frame with an oval window. At the end of the century came art nouveau, which got its name from the shop of the German art dealer Samuel Bing, *La Maison de l'Art Nouveau*, which he opened in Paris in 1895. Mirror frames were designed with sinuous curves and snake-like plant designs embossed on copper and pewter mounts. The Café Lipp, in Paris, has art nouveau tiling from floor to ceiling, and beautiful plain dark wooden frames define the mirrors and the tile pictures and isolate them from the background tiles. Tiles look very fine in wooden frames.

Near the turn of the century, artists themselves began a revolution and like the Renaissance artists, many grew interested in creating distinctive frames for their own pictures. They are usually designed solely with the picture in mind and with no thought to the settings in which they might find themselves.

The Pre-Raphaelites in England designed many of their own frames, harking back to Italian fifteenth-century frames with classical proportions, carved and gilded in the spirit of William Morris's belief in the traditional pride of the craftsman. Rossetti used Gothic columns and a painted predella for his *The Blessed Damozel*, now in the Lever Collection, Port Sunlight, USA. He painted six replicas of the original of *Beata Beatrix* (1872, in the Tate Gallery, London), and one of them has a frame with a predella painting showing the meeting of *Dante and Beatrice in Paradise* (to be seen in the Art Institute of Chicago).

James McNeill Whistler designed and decorated various frames, usually gilded or painted black, and reeded, with his butterfly emblem incorporated somewhere on one of the sides of the frame. The carved reeding or painted patterns that he used were often not symmetrical but were related to the composition of his picture. There is one of these frames in the Tate Gallery (*Old Battersea Bridge*).

The French impressionists were moved to make their own frames in a completely new vein; plain white frames were popular. In the 1880s, Georges Seurat continued the pointillism from his pictures over his frames, and sometimes painted a narrow border on the picture itself. The frame and border were painted, as he described, 'in the harmony opposed to those of the tones, colours and lines of the picture', and this accentuated the luminosity of the painting itself. The two paintings he exhibited as a pair in Paris and Brussels, of Le Crotoy (looking upstream in one, downstream in the other), were the first he treated in this manner, and he then used the same idea on many of the paintings he had made before then, in some cases painting the border over the edge of the already painted canvas or board.

The twentieth century, in efforts to break from the past, has produced many experiments in framing to suit the great variety of painting and environment. Most of the frames are plain. Glass is no longer considered necessary for the protection of oil paintings, as it had been in the nineteenth century. John Singer Sargent and others displayed their work in antique frames that had been stripped to the bare wood and left to look worn. In 1924 Max Ernst attached actual objects to his frame for *Two Children Are Threatened by a Nightingale*: a wooden gate, a house, a knob. Magritte's painting *La Représentation* in the Penrose Collection, London, which he painted in 1937, has a narrow simple gilt frame moulded to the outline of the painting, which is the curve

The Owl and the Pussycat *by Peter Blake. The distinctive frame is very much part of the picture it frames.*

of a torso. Peter Blake has experimented with many different types of frame, including old ones that he has found and others that he has had made. *The Owl and the Pussycat*, which he painted in 1981–3 and which hangs in Bristol Museum and Art Gallery, has a copper frame with embossed boat on a sea with setting sun, and he has taken the shape of this boat to use in his picture.

In his series of fairy paintings each has its own distinctive frame very different from the others and very much part of the picture it frames.

As well as considering the styles of the past, it is worth looking at contemporary fashion and materials. Modern mouldings in metal and wood add great variety to the stock of picture-frame moulding already available.

2   TYPES OF FRAMES

There are so many different types of frames that it is not possible in a book of this size to describe them all. I have selected a few models that can be attempted by the beginner—and which can be improved upon by the more practised frame-maker. Here is a summary of some suitable frames for different types of display, including oil and watercolour painting, posters and reproductions, needlework and fabric, photographs and three-dimensional frames for objects.

OIL AND ACRYLIC PAINTINGS

Oils and acrylics are generally painted on canvas, usually supported on a wooden stretcher. When measuring these it is important to take into account the extra dimension of the canvas that has been stretched around the edges of the support. Thick canvas might make 6 mm (¼ in) difference in measurement to each side.

If you are using a deep moulding, then the depth will be adequate to hold the canvas and stretcher. On the less deep mouldings it will be necessary to add some clips or nails to support the stretcher.

The artist may have painted directly on to a panel. This could be a manufactured canvas panel (available at most art shops in a number of sizes), or a wooden panel, or some composite material such as chipboard or hardboard. These panels are sometimes coated with gesso (see page 66), or primed with special paint.

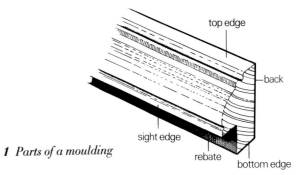

1 Parts of a moulding

A basic frame

Care must be taken with paintings not to cover up too much of the edge with a wide rebate. Some paintings are better presented with all edges exposed. The simplest way to do this is to attach small, thin pieces of wood to the outside of the painting. With canvas over a stretcher they can be mitred and then glued and nailed to the wooden supports. For panel paintings it will first be necessary to make a wooden support for the back, to which the external wooden strip of frame can be attached. The support can be glued to the panel. Many modern paintings—particularly large ones—are presented in this manner, for it provides a minimal neat edge at a very low cost.

Floating frame

For a more interesting and yet still simple appearance, the 'floating frame' is sometimes used—so called as

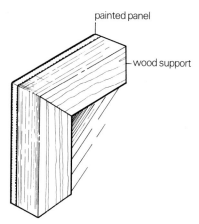

painted panel

wood support

2 A wooden support attached to the back of a panel painting allows the painting to be presented with all edges exposed

the painting appears to float in the recess around it.

For this type of frame it is only necessary to use flat timber. The proportions can vary to suit the picture. Normally the outer edge is at least 1 cm (½ in) higher than the recess, and a little proud of the painting itself. The recess is formed by a step, and this can be made simply by joining, for example, a piece of flat timber 5 cm (2 in) thick to a piece 3 cm (1½ in) thick.

These two pieces form the moulding for the frame and

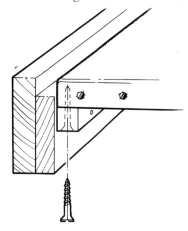

3 Cross section of a floating frame

should be glued and nailed together so that one side is flush. Thin veneer pins placed a few centimetres apart and PVA glue will be sufficiently strong to hold them.

This section is now mitred in the normal way to construct the frame. It may be that the painting will look neater with some thin wooden strips nailed around it as well, in which case this should be done first. The main frame needs to be a tight fit around the edge of the painting, so careful measuring is very important.

To secure the canvas to the frame, small batons at least 1 cm (½ in) square need to be screwed to the back of each side. It is not necessary to have them the entire length of each side—but there should be enough to support the picture. To fix the canvas support, screw through the baton into the stretcher with an appropriately sized screw. Panel paintings, without a wooden support, can be glued straight on to the baton. It is helpful to stick tape on to the back of this type of frame so that no daylight can emerge between the recessed step and the side of the painting.

The recess is more dramatic if painted a matt black, for this will emphasize the shadow around the painting. The outside top edge may be painted or stained to complement the painting and contrast the recess. To achieve a well-painted surface it is a good policy to use a primer and an undercoat on the wood. Then rub this down with fine sandpaper before applying the top coat.

This type of frame works very well with modern paintings—but is also suitable for a whole range of traditional styles. There are many possibilities of colour and dimension to experiment with and the materials are comparatively inexpensive.

Box frame

Another type of frame also suitable for oil and acrylic painting is the box frame. This is a simple box shape around the picture. It can be made to fit flush with the

A simple floating frame. The recess, which is about 2.5 cm (1 in) wide, is painted matt black to give emphasis to the edge of the painting and to echo the black objects in the painting.

The edge of the frame is about 2.5 cm (1 in) higher than the recess and 1 cm (½ in) higher than the canvas. The canvas has been edged with red tape to neaten the edge.

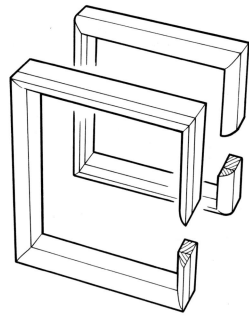

4a *Flush-fitting box frames without a rebate*

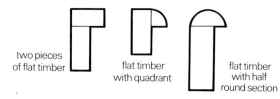

two pieces of flat timber

flat timber with quadrant

flat timber with half round section

4b *Cross section illustrating the different methods of creating a rebate for a box frame*

picture so that no rebate is necessary. Alternatively, a small quadrant, fillet or half-round section can be joined to the timber to create a rebate.

Where no rebate is used, accurate measurement is essential for a tight fit. The painting should be tested for squareness. A simple way to do this is to measure the diagonals. They should be the same; if not, some adjustment will need to be made. The painting can then be attached, in a similar way to the floating frame, by screwing batons to the frame and securing the painting to these.

Again, experiment with dimension and colour. For something dramatic, a simple matt black deep-sided box might be attractive. For more subtle paintings, perhaps a hardwood box in mahogany or oak lightly stained and waxed would be more suitable.

There are a great many shapes of wood that can be bought from timber yards. These may be architraves and beadings for door and window surrounds, or picture rail and dado sections for wall decoration. These can be joined in a vast number of permutations, and experimentation with them constitutes a good exercise for the imagination in design and structure. This method of creating your own picture-frame moulding is frequently more satisfying than buying rebated and finished moulding. For the more advanced carpenter, there are a range of moulding or combination planes that can cut different shapes into flat timber, as well as plough planes for cutting rebates. In recent years hand-held cutting machines, called routers, have been developed for the use of the home-based carpenter. These can be used to cut your own mouldings and shapes, and come with a large variety of cutting blades. Bespoke picture framers frequently have their own spindle mould cutters which are a more powerful variety of the router. However this book is mainly for the beginner and this kind of carpentry skill is best learnt practically. Moreover, there are so many cheap, commercially available wooden moulding shapes that it is hardly necessary to manufacture them.

Wide-margin frame

The example here (fig. 5) is a comparatively simple shape that can be bought from most picture-frame moulding suppliers already cut. However, there may be only certain dimensions available and so it is useful to be able to make your own.

The main feature is the central margin; this is often flat, but can be at an angle or U-shaped. Frequently the latter is called a 'spoon', because of the shape.

To this central piece can be added a deep back edge and a smaller moulding, incorporating a rebate, for the front edge. These should be glued together and can then be taped to hold them in position until the glue has set. They can then be nailed discreetly so that the nails are not exposed. The example in fig. 5 can be made from timber to be found at most good timber yards. It is a 'classical' shape, favoured by sixteenth-century Italian frame-makers and still used today in a variety of dimensions.

The flat border in the middle lends itself to all kinds of elaborate decoration. Alternatively, it can be used as a wide, flat area of colour or stain. The two edges either

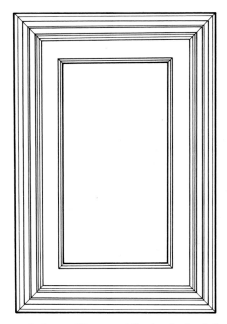

5 A wide margin frame. The central flat border lends itself to many different styles of decoration.

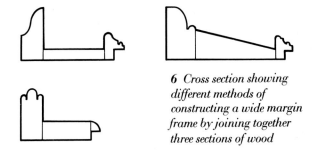

6 Cross section showing different methods of constructing a wide margin frame by joining together three sections of wood

side could be contrasted against the middle or against one another. The Italian Renaissance frames of this kind were frequently painted, embossed or engraved in a decorative manner along the central margin whilst the two edges might be carved and gilded.

These patterns are improved by using gesso as a

7 A corner and centre ornament taken from a Renaissance frame in the National Gallery, London

ground (see pages 66–67 for methods of mixing and applying gesso). The soft gesso can be etched using a bradawl or nail. This throws the pattern into relief and is very effective when painted or gilded. The gesso should be applied carefully over the whole frame or the parts of the frame that are to be painted. If the pattern is to be etched, at least six or seven coats should be applied. The more coats of gesso the deeper the pattern can be etched.

The gesso should be smoothed with fine sandpaper and garnet paper, and then the pattern can be drawn in. A little water applied with a soft brush over the drawn pattern will make it easier to etch with a pointed

A selection of plain wooden mouldings – oak, pine, ramin and mahogany – in a variety of different cuts and sizes.

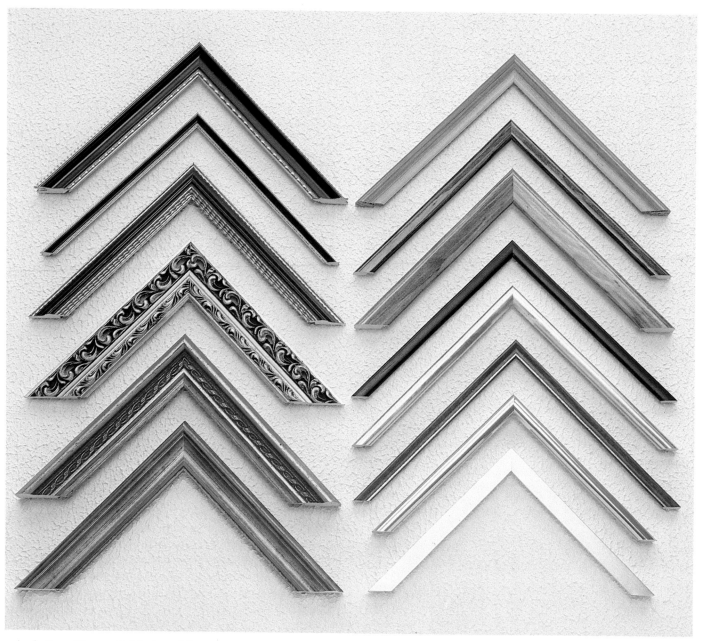

A selection of factory-finished mouldings.

instrument. Too much water will weaken the gesso and cause the cut to go too deep.

There are many fine examples of this 'Florentine' type of frame in the National Gallery, London (see fig. 7). Patterns may be copied from them, traced from books or improvised. They generally have four identical corner ornamented patterns and a smaller central pattern for each side of the frame.

These 'period' frames may not suit all types of picture, but for reproductions of Renaissance paintings or as decorative surrounds for mirrors they are excellent. A modern variation using a similarly shaped moulding can be made by covering the middle section in some sort of fabric. Canvas, hessian, linen or velvet can all be used for this. The cloth can be cut to size and then glued, using fabric glue, on to whatever sections are appropriate.

There are many possible variations using different combinations of moulded pieces together. One of the easiest is to use builder's architrave—this is sometimes called ogee when S-shaped in cross section. These architraves can be adapted for framing by either adding a quadrant to form a rebate on the thick edge or else adding a thin piece of timber to the bottom (fig. 8).

More elaborate structures can be assembled using sections such as simple squares of wood, picture rail, insert moulding, etc. A simple way to start is to make a flat wooden base of, for example, 5×1 cm ($2 \times \frac{1}{2}$ in) timber. To this squares can be added at each corner (see fig. 9). For more decoration, beading, architrave or picture rail can be added between the squares. For a final touch some angled slip moulding can be inserted on the inner edge. This is only one example of the many variations that are possible.

If your mitre saw is capable of cutting the angles, then of course triangles, pentangles, hexagons and octagons can also add variety to the shape and structure of your frames.

8 Builder's architrave can be adapted for framing by creating a rebate. Two methods are illustrated below.

(a) A quadrant can be glued to the side

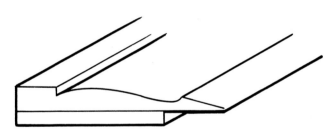

(b) Or a thin, flat piece of timber can be glued to the bottom

In addition to these home-produced types of frame, there are a large number of manufactured mouldings. Some of these are plain wood mouldings, generally pine, ramin, oak or mahogany. These can be finished in many different ways (Chapter 6). There are also mouldings with an industrial surface, commonly in gold, silver and metallic finish, or in lacquer, paint or stain. Great care should be taken in cutting these smooth surfaces, as superficial marks and nicks are difficult and time consuming to repair.

Drawings, watercolours, lithographs and etchings do

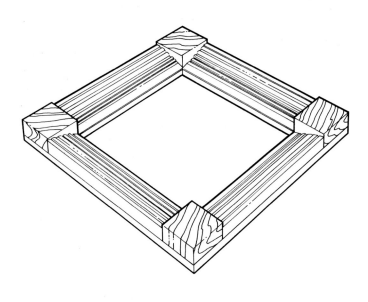

9 *On top of a simple, flat base, squares of timber have been added to the corners; beading or architrave can be used for extra decoration between the squares.*

not need different kinds of moulding, though frequently thinner sections are preferred. Works on paper generally need to be mounted and glazed to protect them more completely. (Mounting is discussed in Chapter 4.)

POSTERS AND PRINTS

For posters, prints and reproductions, thin metallic frames are often favoured. These are of course suitable for all types of work to be framed. Many of the metal mouldings come in kit form and can be assembled at home easily enough by following the instructions. The most common are made of aluminium and sold in pairs of sides, so that you buy two packets for each frame. In this way you should be able to find some that approxi-

mately fit your picture. The mitres have already been cut, so all that is required is to assemble the frame using the angle plates and screws included in the kit. There are other types of kit frame available, commonly the perspex box and the clip frame and glass.

In the range of metallic mouldings there are also some with a thin veneer of metal fixed over a wooden base, giving the appearance of a solid metal frame. These can be cut using ordinary tenon or mitre saws, but repeated use will blunt the blades very rapidly. A 'junior' hacksaw will saw them easily, and should fit into a mitre box. Mitre saws with replaceable blades can be fitted with a hacksaw blade. Care must be taken not to buckle the thin skin of metal through careless manipulation of the saw. The wooden base allows the sides to be glued with PVA and these can be clamped in the normal manner. If you possess an electric drill and a small bit suitable for drilling through metal, then pilot holes can be drilled through the metal into the wood. If you do not have a suitable drill or do not want to have unsightly holes in the side of the frame then an alternative is to cut some right angled triangles of hardboard. Glue and nail these to the back of the frame after the final assembly. In this way the sides of the frame are untouched but the back is securely supported. This device can be used for all frames

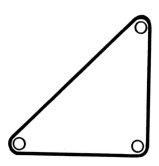

10 *Simple wood or metal triangle*

where you wish to have the sides unblemished. Brass or chrome triangles can be bought with holes already drilled for small screws (see fig. 10).

Posters and reproductions can be framed without a moulding, using clips to hold the glass, picture and a backing board together. The spring metal clips, usually called 'emu' clips, are widely used. They come in a few different sizes to fit small and large pictures. A small hole, the right distance from the edge, must be bored into the backing board. A bradawl is a useful tool for this, and hardboard is suitable for the backing board. This hole takes the tooth of the clip, and the rest is stretched on to the front and held in place with the springy tongue. It is more secure and attractive to have these clips evenly spaced around the edges. It is also advisable to smooth the facing edges of the glass with fine glasspaper to dull the sharpness and prevent cuts to the fingers.

A safer and usually more satisfactory way of making a glass and clip frame is to buy some perspex or metal clips that have a hole drilled through them on one side. These can be screwed to the side of the backing, holding the glass in place. The plywood, hardboard or other composite boards generally used for the back do not receive screws particularly well, and so it is advisable to join wooden batons around the edge of the backing material. These can be glued and nailed, and then when secure the

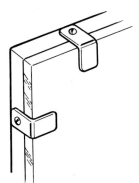

11 *A glass and clip frame showing a metal clip screwed into the side of the wooden base*

clips and screws can be attached to them. This gives an attractive edge to the frame and protects composite board from crumbling at the edges, which it is prone to do.

Normally these 'clip' frames are only used for convenience, speed and economy. They are useful for temporary display in exhibitions or for frequent changes of picture the same size. They do not fully protect the pictures and allow dust and moisture to penetrate between the glass and picture. The 'emu' clips are also prone to jump off under stress, such as when moving the picture from one place to another, making the whole structure unstable.

Posters and prints that are to be displayed without mounts look just as pleasing with a narrow wood or metal frame. These give a minimal edge, so that the picture is presented very simply—but with all the protection of a frame, glass and backing board.

NEEDLEWORK AND EMBROIDERY

Displays of needlework, embroidery, batik or any other decorated fabric present a few problems to the framer.

The fabric does need to be attached to some kind of support. Often wooden stretchers, the same that are used for paintings, are suitable. Most fabric that has a margin can be tensioned in the same way as canvas. It is useful to have special cloth pliers, with extra wide grips, to hold the cloth taut while either tacks or staples are driven into the wooden support. These 'stretchers' can be bought in many sizes from good artists' supply shops—or can be made very simply, using flat timber: butt or mitre joints can be used for these stretchers. For good results in stretching cloth, it is best to turn the frame continually, adding more tacks or staples to each side as you turn, to achieve an equal tension on all sides. For more delicate cloths the stretcher will be too harsh a support. These can be either sewn or glued, using fabric glue, on to card. It is important to shave the sharp edge off the inside dimension of the frame, otherwise it will cause friction and consequently damage to the cloth over a period of years. The square edge needs to be rounded and this can be done very quickly with sandpaper.

Another problem is to keep the fabric away from the surface of the glass; this helps to prevent damage caused by condensation. It can be done, in the same way as with works on paper, by making a window in mount card. This does not always look appropriate, but I have seen it effectively used with thin fabrics such as batik under glass. An alternative is to use 'slip' or 'insert' mouldings. These are placed inside the frame and act as a barrier between the fabric and the glass.

Fig. 12 shows a classic shape of an insert moulding, but there are many alternatives. Some are already covered with linen canvas, hessian or velvet, and can be mitred straight away. It is helpful to cut the cloth with a sharp knife along the line of the cut, prior to sawing, as often the teeth of the saw cause unsightly fraying of the material. Plain wood sections can be decorated with paint, or a complementary coloured fabric can be glued to them.

Slip frames are usually thin strips of wood with a bevelled edge or minimal decoration. Often they are gilded. These do not allow so much of a gap between glass and fabric, because of their thinness, but it is often

12 A shaped insert moulding inside the frame acts as a barrier between the glass and the object

outer frame

glass

shaped insert moulding

fabric

30

sufficient space. They are frequently useful as an extra dimension to a frame, should the window be just a little too big for the picture, and also as a decorative strip within a frame.

It is often easier to assemble the insert moulding after constructing the main frame. In this way the slip can be cut and measured by sight rather than by a ruler. Only a little glue, and perhaps a small pin, is necessary to hold them together. Traditionally they were usually cut so tight that they did not need any joining, and were left without nails or glue, supported within the frame.

These inserts can be used to create a larger volume of space within the frame. This can be very attractive as an effect, and can also be useful for displaying objects.

THREE-DIMENSIONAL FRAMES

Plates, coins, medals, butterflies, jewelry and precious objects can all be protected and displayed handsomely within a frame.

For the thinner three-dimensional objects such as coins and medals, the space created by an insert frame will normally be adequate. For the bulkier objects it will be necessary to construct a small ledge to support the glass at the front of the frame (see fig. 13). A deep moulding or flat timber to which a piece of quadrant can be attached will be necessary. To either of these sections a smaller dimension quadrant or fillet of wood needs to be joined approximately the thickness of the glass away from the rebate. These should be glued and nailed with small veneer pins. Ideally the fillet should be thinner than the rebate above it so that it is almost invisible from the front.

The backing board to which the objects are attached can be screwed to the back of the frame. Alternatively the back can be held by pins in the gap at the bottom of the frame.

The assembly of this kind of frame, sometimes called a

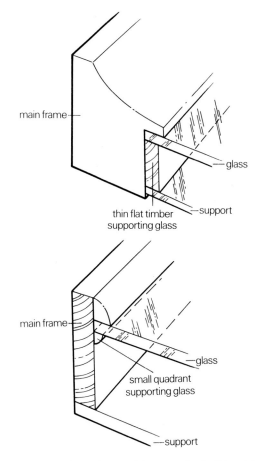

main frame

glass

thin flat timber
supporting glass

support

main frame

glass

small quadrant
supporting glass

support

13 Two methods of creating a wider space for bulkier objects

'shadow box', can be done in this manner. Take the piece of moulding or plain timber with attached rebate, and glue on to it the fillet or quadrant that will hold the glass. This should be the same width away from the rebate all along the moulding. Generally 2 mm (1/16 in) glass is used for picture framing, so that the support for the glass should be a little over 2 mm (1/16 in) away from the rebate. Glue the fillet and then hold it in place with tape until the glue has set. Then it can be nailed for extra safety, taking care to punch the nails below the surface so that they are not visible.

The sides of the frame are then cut from this section. Three sides are joined together first. The fourth side is left open to allow the glass to slide neatly into place. Finally, the fourth side can be put into place. This can be glued and nailed in the usual way or can be screwed into the two adjoining sides with small screws. The holes should be countersunk, so that the screw heads are below the surface. Countersinking attachments can be bought for electric drills, but hand held ones are normally adequate. By using screws in the fourth side, damaged glass can be replaced easily without having to break the frame. The backing board can also be screwed to the main frame to facilitate easy removal or adjustment.

The inside edges of these 'shadow box' frames will be visible so that they must be included in the colour scheme of the whole piece. If a dark shadow is the effect required, the inside edge could be painted matt black or a dark brown. For some exotic moths I once framed, I used a black velvet background and painted the sides matt black. The frame was a dark Jacobean oak colour. The effect was very dramatic, with the colourful moths floating in the darkness surrounded by a deep brown moulding. Many different colour schemes can be employed to enhance all manner of objects.

Fixing the objects to the backing board calls for some ingenuity. For the moths mentioned earlier I used small 1 cm (1/2 in) screws, drilled from the back through the hardboard and velvet. Small pieces of cork (painted matt black) were turned on to the end of the screws. To these the moths were attached by pins pierced through the thorax. This of course is not appropriate for all objects. Jewelry and small items can be sewn, using transparent nylon thread, on to the fabric. Heavier items will probably need to be glued or attached by wire through a hole in the back.

A three-dimensional frame made of ash presenting an antique wedding tiara on red velvet.

These display boxes do enhance the objects presented in a very attractive way, and are used often by jewellers and museums for protection as well as display. By their nature, the boxes are usually deeper than most frames and so some care must be used when hanging them on a wall. The ordinary screw-eye method will tend to make the box droop away from the wall. They are more attractive if they are screwed directly on to a wall. For this purpose it is possible to buy a flush fitting wallplate that can be screwed to both the frame and the picture.

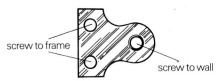

14 *A flush fitting wall plate*

DOUBLE-SIDED FRAMES

There are some objects, documents, drawings or paintings that have something worth looking at on the reverse side. This may be only a small piece, such as a description of the display side, or a signature, in which case a small window can be cut into the backing board and a piece of transparent acetate glued over the window. If, however, the whole of the back needs to be seen, then it should be glazed like the front and perhaps mounted as well. For this it will be necessary to have a reasonably deep moulding that can hold two pieces of glass, two mounts and the picture.

The package can be assembled in the normal way and the glass at the back can be carefully nailed over, using small headless nails. These nails can be covered by tape or ornamental string.

If, however, both sides are equally noteworthy or two photographs want to be seen back to back, a double frame can be made using a rebate at the back as well as the front. Quadrant, slip or an appropriate beading can

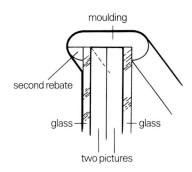

15 *A double-sided frame. The deep moulding contains two pieces of glass, two pictures back-to-back, and a quadrant to create a second rebate.*

be attached using nails. The pictures can then be viewed from either side equally well.

To view both, without having to turn the picture around on a wall, it is quite simple to create a stand from a block of wood. The stand can then be screwed into the frame and some baize glued to the bottom to prevent scratches on table tops. An alternative idea is to place two screw eyes on the top edge of the frame, which it can hang from.

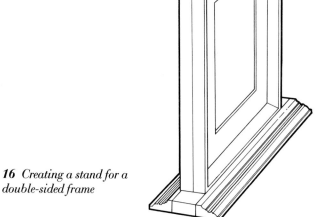

16 *Creating a stand for a double-sided frame*

33

FREE-STANDING FRAMES

Another type of frame that can be used on a table or shelf is the free-standing frame with a 'strut-back' support. This kind of frame is usually for photographs. It is generally small for reasons of space and portability and therefore it is better to use thin, lightweight moulding and only a narrow mount. Small fastenings can be bought for the back that can be turned through 90°, allowing the back and the photos to come out easily.

There are a number of ways of making 'strut-back' supports for the frame. First cut the strut from a piece of card or hardboard. It should be approximately two-thirds of the height of the frame and wider at one end than at the other. One way to do this is to cut a triangle of card and then cut it down to the required size. These struts can then be joined to the backing board using fabric tape or a small cabinet hinge. A piece of ribbon can be fastened between the back and the strut to hold the frame at the required angle.

This kind of frame can look very attractive with fabric or leather as a surface.

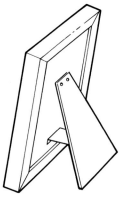

17 Strut-back frame

FABRIC FRAMES

Pleasing finishes can be made with fabric—either for mounts or frames. They are obviously not as durable as wood or metal, but will last for some years.

A simple fabric-covered frame I have seen was a pale green hessian fabric glued over a flat wooden section with a narrow, raised, gilded rebate. This was used with a delicately coloured oriental painting under glass. The texture of the hessian was a pleasant contrast to the smooth quality of the silk under glass.

There are so many fabrics with which to experiment. In general they can be glued on to wood using a latex fabric glue. Canvas, linen, felt, velvet or silk can all be used for their distinctive texture and quality. The material should be clean and preferably ironed prior to gluing, for creases are sometimes difficult to smooth out. It is normal practice to glue the fabric on to the individual sides of a frame before assembly. Where there are awkward overhangs, separate pieces of fabric can be attached before the main fabric is glued.

It is possible to make a fabric frame without wood. As a substitute, cotton wadding or some suitable stuffing can be used. First cut the shape of the frame in card, and then cut the window out of the middle. Lay the material down on a clean flat surface. Place the card on top, and cut the window out of the fabric, leaving a margin to fold around the edges of the board.

Make diagonal cuts in the corners of the fabric, and fold and glue the inner margins to the back of the board (see fig. 18). At this stage it is possible to pad out the frame with cotton wadding. This gives it a greater thickness and enhances the soft contours of a fabric frame. Lastly, make diagonal cuts to the external corners of the fabric, and fold and glue them to the back.

A backing board can be cut to the same size and glued along the bottom and two sides. This creates a sleeve into which some light perspex or transparent plastic can be fitted. Glass may be too heavy and sharp for this frame.

When making a 'strut-back' fabric frame, the same or a contrasting fabric can be attached to the back and the strut for an attractive finish.

The portrait: a floating frame. The landscape: a finished moulding with a colour wash on the spoon recess.

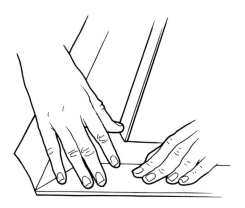

18 The fabric frame: make diagonal cuts in the corners of the fabric; fold and glue to the back of the board.

There are now many new types of metal moulding, from the very thin, elegant coloured ones, to the more glossy gold and silver finished varieties. These are generally kit-frames complete with angle plates and instructions for assembly, though whole lengths and the necessary accessories can be bought from a good supplier. The kits are available in packs of two sides, so that two packs will make a four-sided frame. In this way it is possible to choose dimensions very close to your picture size. Another metal style of moulding consists of a thin skin of metal stretched over a wooden base. These come in a wide variety of styles and finishes, and can be handled in the same way as ordinary wooden moulding, except that you will need a hacksaw to cut through them.

In addition to the stock of contemporary moulding designs, there are also lots of 'instant' frames to be found in department stores, stationery shops and framing accessory suppliers. These come in stock sizes and are pre-fitted with glass, hardboard, swing clips, and strut-backs. There are also ready-made frames, from the large, often rather gaudy ornamental pseudo period style frames, usually in a gold finish, to the more simple plain or lacquered wood varieties. Glass, mounts and backing boards can be fitted easily to these supports, and extra decoration can be added to the surface of the frame or the mount to complement the picture.

In general these 'instant' frames are useful to those who do not want to make their own frames, but less than satisfying to those who wish to develop practical skills and an aesthetic sense.

3   TOOLS AND MATERIALS

In discussion of tools and materials necessary for frame making it is important to realize that there is a whole range of items available, some of which are appropriate for the beginner and some which are more for the needs of the professional. If one can afford the tools of the professional, they are usually more precise and sometimes easier to use. If not, there are many ways to improvise and many inexpensive processes for finishing frames in a decorative manner.

MITRE BOX

The most fundamental tool necessary is a mitre box. Not all frames need to be mitred, and straight butt joins can be used quite effectively with flat timber. When using moulding, though, the mitre is the only join worth considering.

Mitre boxes comes in all sorts of shapes and sizes; the most basic and cheapest are the wooden boxes. These usually have two 45° cuts and a 90° straight cut. They can be bought quite cheaply from most good tool shops, or made at home using a protractor and spare timber. With a good sharp tenon saw they will give you reasonably good mitre corners. Their main disadvantage is that the saw guides become worn and therefore the margin of error is increased to the point where your mitres are no longer good enough. The more expensive mitre boxes come with metal or plastic flanges to protect the cuts, and these do last longer.

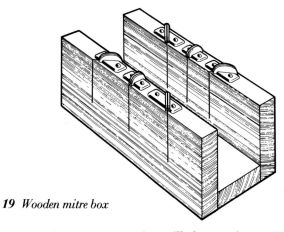

19 Wooden mitre box

Slightly more expensive still, but easier to use, is the metal mitre box. This usually comes with two screw clamps that can be used to hold the wood in place whilst cutting, and later on can also be used as a corner clamp.

For both types of box it will be necessary to buy a tenon saw. These vary enormously in quality and price. The thinner the blade the easier it is to trim off small quantities of wood. A tenon saw with a good quality thin steel blade, with at least five teeth to the centimetre (twelve per inch), and a comfortable handle that matches the depth of your mitre box, is best.

Also available is a metal mitre box with small dowelling pegs that can be moved to different positions on the metal table. This enables the user to make many different angle cuts, and so be able to make octagonal,

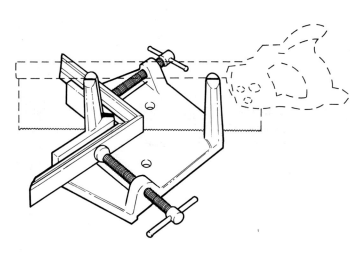

20 *Metal mitre box that can also be used as a corner clamp*

hexagonal, pentagonal and triangular frames as well as the conventional rectangle.

MITRE SAW

For the more persistent amateur who thinks that he or she might want to continue to make frames, there are a number of mitre saws on the market. These vary a great deal in size, but are quite similar in principle. Because of the fixed angle (the shaft is secured in a ratchet) and a very thin saw blade, these mitre saws will give you very precise mitres and. enable you to shave off minute amounts of wood. However, even the cheapest are probably out of the range of most beginners, so this is perhaps not a tool to be bought straight away.

Most professional framers use a 'morso' cutter, a foot-operated V-shaped block cutter that gives very precise 45° angles, but these are bulky and very expensive. There are also electric power tools with angle adjustments that can be used for mitres.

It is possible for a skilled carpenter or cabinet-maker to cut an angled mitre by drawing out the angle and cutting straight through the wood, but for a beginner it is essential to use a mitre box and suitable saw.

VICE

Many professional picture framers use a vice, usually built into their workbench, for joining mitre corners. An ordinary metal vice can be adapted for this procedure. After securing the vice to the workbench or table, thin pieces of plywood, hardboard or even cardboard should be attached to the inner sides of the vice to prevent damage to the wooden mouldings when under pressure.

By clamping one side of a frame in the vice with the mitre protruding, another can be glued to it and drilled. It is necessary to have an electric drill for this procedure, so that you can hold the second length of moulding in the correct position whilst drilling. The drill hole should pierce both sides, so that there is a minimum of nailing. It does take a little practice to keep the two sides in register throughout. Repeat the procedure with the other two sides. Later, when the two L-shapes are ready to join together, they can be fixed in turn using the vice again and a prop for the opposite corner.

RULER OR TAPE MEASURE

The next most important tool on the list is a ruler. Many different types exist—metal, wood, or perspex. It is advisable to have one at least 45 cm (18 in) long and preferably a metre rule. A ruler can be easier to use than a tape measure, simply because you can hold it in place more easily along the length of a piece of moulding. Correct and accurate measuring is the very essence of good picture framing, and it is very worth while to invest in a good quality ruler. The perspex ones have the added advantage of being transparent and therefore are useful for drawing out the lines for mount cutting.

Left top-reverse moulding projects the picture forwards. **Right** recessed in a frame of lime wood.

HAMMER

A tack hammer or any small hammer is essential. If larger hammers are used they can very easily split or damage delicate mouldings. These are not very expensive and can of course be used for other do-it-yourself purposes.

NAIL PUNCH

This is used for knocking the nail heads below the surface of the wood, so that wood stopper can be used to fill the nail holes for a neater, more professional appearance. These are available in a variety of sizes from most ironmongers and tool shops: a good shape to get is one with a recessed head, so that it fits over the nail head to be hit. They are easier to use than the flat or pointed varieties. There is also room for improvisation, as a good stout 10 cm (4 in) screw or nail can be flattened on the point to provide a very reasonable punch.

21 *Recessed nail punch*

DRILLS AND BRADAWLS

In order to nail more easily a drill or bradawl can be used to make the pilot holes. The bradawl is usually made of hardened steel and has a wooden or plastic handle above a steel spike a few centimetres long. These make holes prior to nailing. A small hole to a depth of 3–6 mm (⅛–¼ in) is sufficient for softwoods. When using hardwoods you may find that the bradawl does not make much impact, so use either a hand-drill or an electric drill.

CRAMPS AND CLAMPS

Again, there are many types available from most good tool shops. For the beginner who does not want to spend much and will attempt improvisation, strong cord or a large rubber band will clamp most simple frames sufficiently. These can be wedged for extra tension.

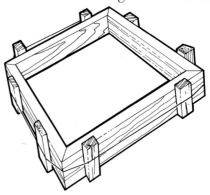

22 *Method of joining frame using wedges with strong cord or a large rubber band*

An inexpensive option is a kit of cord with small plastic corners and a device for holding taut the end of the cord. This costs only a few pounds and is easy to use.

Slightly more sophisticated, the Elwood clamp (see fig. 23) has metal corners and a screw tightened for tension using thin metal cable. The metal corner pieces have detachable footplates so that they can be used as corners half way up a deep box frame. This form of clamp is best recommended for the beginner, as it is suitable for all frames and allows for complete assembly in one procedure. Holes are provided in the corners to allow nailing whilst the frame is held tight.

Metal corner cramps (see fig. 24) are an alternative to the string or wire method described above. At least two are necessary and four preferable. If you have a metal mitre box you can use that as one of your cramps. Using four cramps, the whole frame can be assembled dry (without glue) in

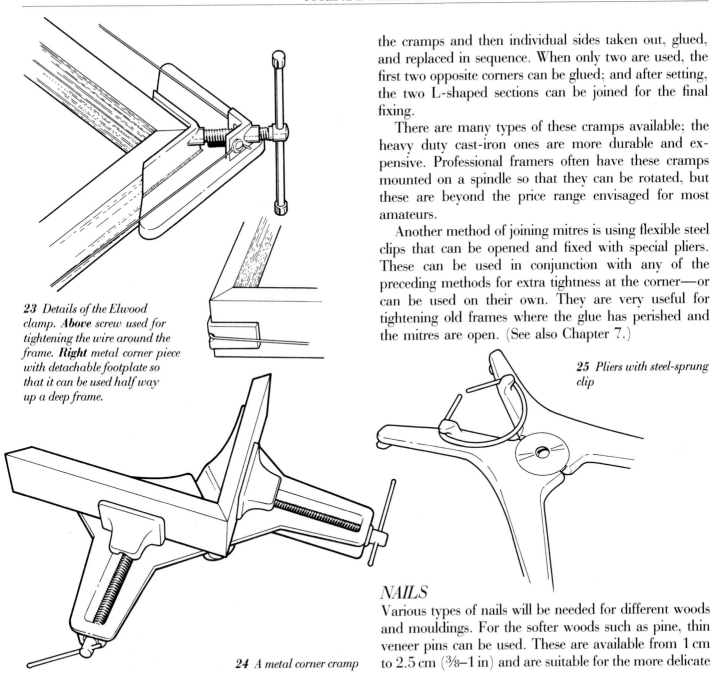

the cramps and then individual sides taken out, glued, and replaced in sequence. When only two are used, the first two opposite corners can be glued; and after setting, the two L-shaped sections can be joined for the final fixing.

There are many types of these cramps available; the heavy duty cast-iron ones are more durable and expensive. Professional framers often have these cramps mounted on a spindle so that they can be rotated, but these are beyond the price range envisaged for most amateurs.

Another method of joining mitres is using flexible steel clips that can be opened and fixed with special pliers. These can be used in conjunction with any of the preceding methods for extra tightness at the corner—or can be used on their own. They are very useful for tightening old frames where the glue has perished and the mitres are open. (See also Chapter 7.)

23 Details of the Elwood clamp. **Above** screw used for tightening the wire around the frame. **Right** metal corner piece with detachable footplate so that it can be used half way up a deep frame.

25 Pliers with steel-sprung clip

NAILS

Various types of nails will be needed for different woods and mouldings. For the softer woods such as pine, thin veneer pins can be used. These are available from 1 cm to 2.5 cm (⅜–1 in) and are suitable for the more delicate

24 A metal corner cramp

mouldings. For harder woods such as oak, ramin or mahogany, something stronger will be required. Steel panel pins or round or oval wire nails should be sufficient. A good pair of pliers incorporating a wire cutting facility is very useful, so that you can trim off nails to suit the size of your frame. It is better to use nails with small heads so that they can be punched below the surface more easily.

GLUE

There are many types of glue for sticking wood. The most universal is polyvinyl adhesive (PVA), a white glue, though usually transparent when dry. Normal drying time is a few hours, but recently rapid hardeners have been added so that it is now possible to get one-hour setting glue or even thirty-minute glue.

For very durable items such as frames or wood joins for outside use there are epoxy resins. These are almost impossible to break when set. Super-rapid-setting glue is very strong but will not usually allow sufficient time to get the corners into alignment.

Animal or 'Scotch' glues, such as are traditionally used for furniture making, prove useful should you need to dismantle a frame, for a hot knife inserted into the mitre will melt the glue. However, for convenience and strength the PVA glues are now preferred and are perfectly strong enough for most types of frame.

KNIFE

A sharp knife is essential for all kinds of mount cutting and also for hardboard or backing board. Again there are many types available.

For precise mount cutting a knife with replaceable blades is useful. Both the craft knives or surgical scalpels are widely used, but there are many modern innovations. It is important to buy one with a comfortable handle so that strong, controlled cuts can be made.

For cutting mounts, a steel straight edge, preferably a metre long with a generous bevel, is necessary. Modern varieties incorporate a rubber tread to prevent movement whilst cutting which is very helpful. (There is more information on the equipment needed for mount cutting in Chapter 4.)

GLASS CUTTER

There is no reason why beginners should not try their hand at cutting glass. Small offcuts are easy to find and practise on.

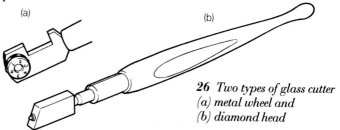

26 *Two types of glass cutter (a) metal wheel and (b) diamond head*

Various types of glass cutters are available, with either a diamond head or a metal wheel. Diamond cutters are expensive, but they last for a long time. Ordinary, metal-wheel cutters do not last long, nor do they cut so easily. Tungsten-hardened metal wheels are probably the most useful. With good care, they last a long time, they are easy to use, and do not cost as much as the diamond type of cutter. The more expensive ones have comfortable wooden handles and replaceable cutting heads; the cheaper ones are disposable.

GLAZING GUN

When fitting backing board into a frame, a glazing gun is a great help. This device shoots small thin diamond-shaped arrows into the wood. It is a fairly expensive item and not essential, since small nails or brads will do just as well—but it does provide a very neat and quick way of fastening the glass and backing board to the frame.

FASTENINGS

There are many different types of fastening for the back of a frame, the most commonly used being the screw eye or the screw eye with ring, usually available in brass or steel in varying sizes to suit the frame in question. With the help of a bradawl these can be easily screwed into the back of a frame.

The D ring and triangular hangers are both attached to the backing board, which for these will need to be hardboard. Small diagonal cuts are made a third of the way down the board; the clips are then inserted through the board, the flaps opened and hammered flat. These allow the frames to hang nearer the wall.

For flush fitting to a wall, small brass plates, commonly called glass or mirror plates, can be screwed to the frame leaving one opening to be screwed, in the opposite direction, to the wall.

Other items useful in a frame-making workshop are pliers, a screwdriver, sandpaper of different grades, wood-fillers, a wood-plane, chisels, files, and masking and gummed tapes.

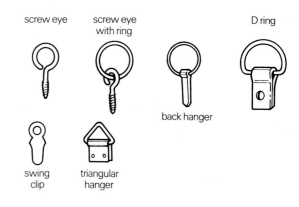

27 Fastenings

To begin frame making you will require most of the tools here described, in one variety or another. Some can be improvised, others will need to be purchased. Second-hand tools are often very good and well made, and can still be found on market stalls and in junk shops. Other, less basic pieces of equipment needed will be described with the relevant procedure in later chapters.

4   MOUNTS AND MOUNT CUTTING

Paintings, drawings and prints on paper need some sort of protection, even if they are being kept in a drawer or portfolio. Normally this is provided by a cut-out mount that is laid over the picture and fixed to it using gummed tape. This presents the picture well, and protects it from rough handling. In a frame it also separates the picture from the glass and therefore prevents damage due to condensation.

There is a very wide range of colour, size and thickness for mount board. The thickness is normally described as 4, 6, 10 or 12 sheet. 4 sheet is the most commonly available in most art and graphic supply shops. Usually there are some colours also available in 6 sheet. 10 or 12 sheet are harder to find, and you will have to locate a specialist shop, or a thicker board can be made quite easily by gluing two boards of a 4 or 6 sheet together with PVA or strong paper glue. These thicker boards give attractive deep bevels but are consequently more difficult to cut. The sizes vary from imperial and double imperial, to new metric measurements. In general, however, the coloured boards are approximately $760 \times 510\,mm$ $(30 \times 20\,in)$.

In addition to the more commercially available boards, there are also 'acid-free' or 'museum quality' boards. These are usually only available in a limited colour range of white, ivory, grey and beige. However, with their increasing popularity a greater variety of colour is becoming available.

Most mount boards that are not labelled as 'acid-free' are made from unrefined groundwood pulp, and are potentially harmful to works on paper. This may take some years to become manifest. It is a wise precaution, therefore, to protect pictures, maps, documents, etc., of any value with 'acid-free' board. Unfortunately these boards are twice the price of ordinary mount board, and a little tougher to cut. 'Acid-free' tape and special glues (Cellofas 'B' grade) are also available for conservation of valuable items. For more precise information, there is an information sheet on the subject of mounting (IS No. 12, 1972) available from the Museums Association. This includes a list of stockists and some useful tips on mount cutting. Good quality artists' supply shops generally carry a range of these boards.

PROPORTION

The next question to consider is the proportions of the margin around the window of the mount.

Some pictures are better presented by a wide margin of mount, particularly small etchings or miniature watercolours. These may need the extra display around them to focus attention. Normally you can get quite a good idea by holding your picture to the mount board and moving it about until you find the optimum width. The extra width normally seen at the bottom of a mount (fig. 28) lifts the picture into focus. Without this extra margin, the bottom tends to look narrower than the other

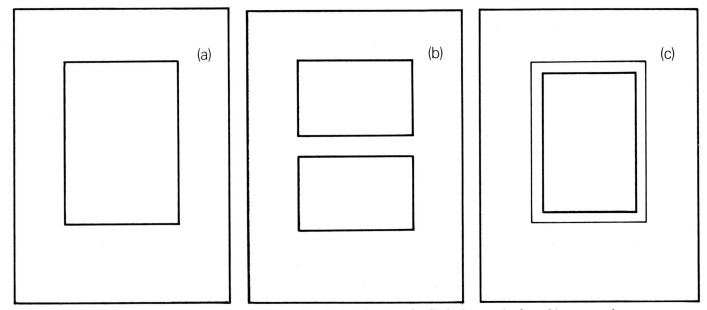

28 *Examples of mounts: (a) the single mount; (b) the double-windowed mount, for displaying a pair of matching or complementary pictures; (c) the double mount, usually cut from two different colour mount boards.*

three sides. There are no rules for dimensions, but it is worth mentioning that even the untutored eye picks up a small discrepancy in width very easily. An extra centimetre on a 5 cm margin, for example, is enough.

A double-windowed mount can be attractive for a pair of matching or complementary pictures. For the more ambitious beginner, a multi-windowed mount is an interesting and economical way of presenting a collection of photographs, paintings or cards. These need to be drawn and cut carefully, for a mistake in the wrong direction of a bevel can ruin an hour's work.

MEASURING AND CUTTING

Before cutting a mount it is first necessary to make accurate measurements. For the beginner who is not used to working in precise measurements, this may be difficult. With practice, concentration and double checking, mistakes can be avoided.

Check the corners of your mount board for 'squareness' before beginning to cut. For this either a set square or, perhaps easier, a circular protractor is used.

Do not assume anything to be square—even pre-cut mount board. To find a true square place a ruler along the side of the mount, and place the 90° set square against it. Draw the right angle; it is now possible to establish the other three. A quick way to check the 'squareness' of a mount or a frame is to measure the diagonals. If the angles are all 90°, the diagonals will be the same.

Take as an example a picture of 25×20 cm (10×8 in)—height is usually before width—and allowing a margin on the sides and top of 5 cm (2 in), and 6 cm (2½ in) on the bottom. Before marking out, you may find it useful to draw a rough diagram of the mount and window with all the measurements indicated.

It is wise to allow at least 2 mm (1⁄16 in) on each side as

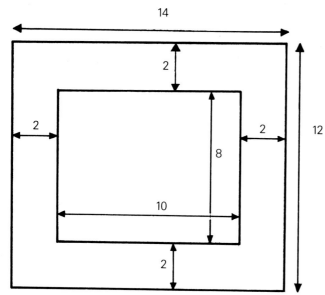

29 *Diagram of mount with measurements indicated*

an overlap, so the picture can be taped easily to the sides of the mount. With the 'overlap allowance' reducing the height and width of the window by 4 mm (⅛ in) each, the actual measurements will be 24.6 × 19.6 cm (9⅞ × 7⅞ in). From this, calculate the overall dimensions of the mount by adding on the margins—6 cm (2½ in) for the bottom and 5 cm (2 in) for the other three sides.

Overall height: 24.6 + 5 + 6 cm = 35.6 cm
   (9⅞ + 2 + 2½ in = 14⅜ in)
Overall width: 19.6 + 5 + 5 cm = 29.6 cm
   (7⅞ + 2 + 2 in = 11⅞ in).

Mark this out on the mount board and cut using a straight edge and knife. For this square cut, use the flat side of the straight edge. In the beginning it is better to cut two or three times rather than exerting a lot of pressure with the knife. Some very bad cuts to the hands can be sustained with a knife and straight edge. Always be careful to keep the hand holding the straight edge well away and out of the cutting line of the knife.

When the overall size has been cut, mark out the margin all the way round. Connect all the lines and then check for accuracy. The inner window should measure 24.6 × 19.6 cm (9⅞ × 7⅞ in) and all the corners should be 90°.

Cutting the window

It is possible to cut a straight-sided window in the mount in the same way as the outside edge was cut, using knife and flat side of the straight edge. This does not look as attractive as a bevelled edge but is much quicker and easier to make.

There are three main ways to cut bevels in the window of a mount. The most widely used by professional framers these days is an industrial mount cutter. This has a metal track set at 45° attached to a baseboard. A weighted metal runner with replaceable blade runs smoothly along the track. They are easy to use and give uniform bevels and incised corners, but are very expensive.

The second method is with a hand-held cutter. These come in many forms and more seem to be developed every year. The classic hand mount cutter is available in metal or plastic and it holds a replaceable blade at an adjustable angle and depth, tightened with a screw. It has a top edge moulded to the shape of a hand so it can be pushed easily along a straight edge.

It is awkward to hold a straight edge with one hand and push the cutter along with the other. It is made easier by clamping the straight edge to a table or board with a couple of G clamps. However, they have to be adjusted for each cut. With a little time and effort it is possible to construct a simple jig. This makes it much easier to control the cutter, and is particularly useful for large mounts where it is difficult to control both straight edge and cutter over a long distance.

A variety of mounts. Some have been decorated with lines and washes.

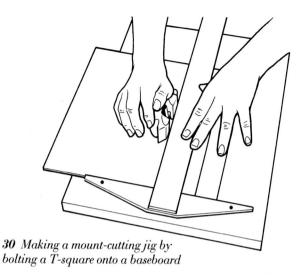

30 *Making a mount-cutting jig by bolting a T-square onto a baseboard*

As mentioned earlier, a fundamental feature of most industrial mount cutters is that they have the metal straight edge mounted on to a baseboard. This can be achieved simply by bolting a T-square on to a plywood or chipboard base.

1   Cut the baseboard to the size of the T-square, leaving a small extra margin.
2   Clamp the T-square on to the centre of the base and test for 'squareness'.
3   Using a metal drill bit, drill holes for bolts. Make sure that you drill vertically through the T-square into the base, as any angle will alter the squareness. Drill holes on each side of the T and one or two at the end of the arm.
4   Using butterfly nuts or suitable bolts and washers, secure the T-square to the base. Check again for squareness.
5   It may be that the end of the arm will need padding underneath to make it level with the other end. A small piece of hardboard can be fitted and drilled through at the same time.

When using the jig it is much better to have a protective card underneath. This protects the baseboard and the sharp end of the blade. This simple jig will enable you to cut more easily and therefore more accurately. With a little pressure the T-square should bend to hold the mount in place as you push the cutter along. Make sure you move the protective card in between cuts so that the blade does not catch in a previous cut, as this will cause stiffness and a rough cut.

In some cutters the blade is positioned slightly away from the edge of the block. It is useful to have a piece of card cut out to this measurement, to use as a marker to align the straight edge the correct distance from the line on the mount.

With practice, it is possible to cut good bevels with a hand-held cutter, and for the beginner these are a worthwhile investment.

To cut a window in a piece of mount board using a knife does require a lot of practice and patience, but when mastered, this skill allows you to cut mounts quickly and accurately.

It is possible to adjust the jig above, in order to use it with a bevelled rule for handcutting with a knife. The equipment needed is a steel straight edge, preferably 1 m (3 ft) long with a wide bevel. More expensive types come with a rubber tread on the bottom, which makes it much easier to hold in place. The other requirement is a mount-cutting knife. There are all kinds of knives suitable for the job. It is important to have a comfortable handle and a sharp replaceable blade, or at least a sharpening stone to maintain the blade. The ordinary type of handicraft knife is too cumbersome for the job. However there are plenty of small craft knives or scalpels, some with plastic or metal handles, and many different blades that can be used.

It is essential to practise bevel cutting on scrap card before attempting a mount. When cutting by hand you can cut from either front or back. It is less messy to draw out on the back, but just ensure that the bevel is sloping in the right direction; it is very easy to make a mistake when working in reverse.

To start, pierce the card at one corner of the window and, keeping an even angle using the bevel on the rule, draw the knife along. If you are using a lightweight knife (such as a scalpel), you can check the angle of cut by taking your hand off the knife and observing the angle of penetration. It will almost certainly be necessary to make two or three cuts. (With practice and a substantial knife it is possible to cut in one stroke.) Try making a shallow pilot cut on the first stroke. This will make it easier for the subsequent cuts to run in the same bevel. Too much strain and pressure when starting will cause the straight edge to move and so give imperfect results. Until practice has made hand-cutting easier, it will be necessary to cut in the corners with a razorblade or sharp knife. Smooth any imperfections on the bevel with fine sandpaper.

Cutting a curve

One advantage of a hand-held mount cutter is that it can be used for cutting a circular or an oval mount. The larger the oval or circle, the easier it is to cut the curves—ovals with a height of less than 10 cm (4 in) will be difficult to cut.

1 Decide upon the size of the oval
2 Rule out the measurements onto thick card
3 Calculate half the measurement of the longest line. Measuring from the end of the shortest line, mark off this amount on the longest line, top and bottom.
4 Insert a pin at both these points
5 Place a piece of thread round one pin. Tie a knot in the thread at the far end of the longest line.
6 Put a pencil inside the loop. Pull the thread taut and begin to draw the oval.

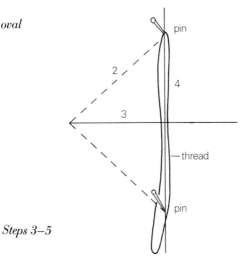

31 Marking out an oval

Steps 3–5

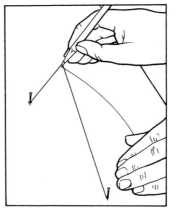

Step 6

For these curved cuts it is necessary to make a template of thick card (fig. 31). This can be cut straight sided and then smoothed with sandpaper. This will make it easier to use as a guide for the cutter. Keeping the template firmly in place, move the cutter slowly around it (see fig. 32).

To cut an oval or circle by hand is quite a skill, and is really not worth learning for a beginner. There are specialist machines for cutting ovals, and a lot of industrially cut sizes are available from graphic supply shops.

A watercolour in a plain ivory mount, with a thin silver leaf on a red-painted spoon frame.

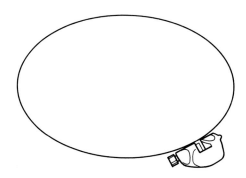

32 Template and hand-held cutter

DECORATING MOUNTS

The traditional style of mount decoration is a neutral or lightly tinted board with bands of light watercolour wash, and lines of varied tones in ink. These generally do look better on 'period' watercolours, etchings, etc., and do not usually suit modern compositions. However, simple lines in a variety of colours can enhance modern work.

It is difficult, in theory, to hit upon a suitable mount colour for a particular picture, and it is made easier by holding the picture against a variety of mounts to consider for a few minutes the complementary effects. It is often impossible to match a predominant colour in the picture with the colour of the mount board. Either a complementary or a contrasting one may be the solution. So as not to dominate the picture, neutral boards of off-white, cream, pale greys and beige are often used. They can also carry decorative lines and washes more effectively.

It is helpful to look at collections of watercolours and prints in museums, galleries and shops to find out different ideas for proportions and colour combinations.

Mark lightly in a hard pencil (2H) around the mount the lines and bands required. (Templates of acetate can be used as guides with pin holes in corner positions.)

To achieve a smooth, evenly tinted wash around a mount does take some practice. To make it easier dampen the area to be painted with water, prior to painting. A soft sable as large as the band requires is the most suitable, but there are cheaper alternatives. Some framers recommend distilled water to mix with the watercolour for more even results. Paint in the band with as few strokes as possible. If colour collects in corners or elsewhere it can sometimes be removed by squeezing the brush dry and lifting the excess colour by dabbing lightly (the dry brush absorbs the wet watercolour like blotting paper).

For lines, a nibbed or lining pen is useful. The lining pen can be adjusted to give a variety of thickness in the line.

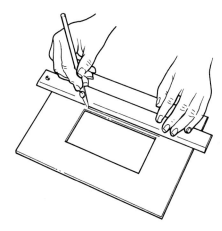

33 Using a lining pen

There are a large variety of water-soluble inks available including gold and silver. They are much easier to use when diluted. In this way subtle tones of sepia and grey may be found, from stronger colours.

To prevent smudging of inked lines, use your ruler upside down; this will separate its edge from the mount. Many of the new perspex set squares and rulers come with a recessed lip on one side for this purpose. Take care

51

not to overshoot the corners with the lines; again, a perspex ruler helps you to spot the corners more easily. When dry, the watercolour washes can be lined along the edges to give a neat, straight line.

There are all sorts of fibre-tip pens, crayons and pencils in a massive range of colour and width that can be used to enhance a mount. For the more austere effect, a simple black or grey line serves to emphasize the picture a little.

Another method of decoration is to use fine papers, marbled, tinted or textured. These can be cut to size and mitred at 45° using a protractor, then lightly glued around the window using paper glue. Self-adhesive or gummed gold strip can be attached. These are often too bright and may need toning down with a stain or ink.

For more elaborate finishes, material such as hessian,

linen, velvet or silk may be stretched and glued on to the mount. This is a very beautiful way to mount something old or exotic, but can work well also with contemporary work. The fabric must be carefully glued using either a latex fabric glue or fabric contact adhesive. The material should be ironed before fixing, to eliminate creases. At the window it should be cut neatly at the corners, and folded and glued on to the reverse side of the mount. After gluing, the board should be weighted to make sure it is evenly glued.

DOUBLE OR TRIPLE MOUNTS

An attractive way of using a brightly coloured mount board without overpowering the subject is to create a double mount. A black and white drawing or etching, for example, may be enhanced by a very thin band of bright red against a wider margin of ivory mount.

Triple mounts are also effective for combining colours. A document or citation that is a little dull on its own may be improved with an 8 cm (3 in) wide outer margin of middle grey, a 4 cm (1½ in) centre margin of a paler grey, and a 5 mm (¼ in) margin of vibrant blue or green.

Obviously there are countless combinations of widths and colours to complement pictures. One difficulty to bear in mind when using more than one mount is that small errors in cutting that would not show on a single mount become all too obvious on a double or triple mount. Double checking for accuracy of angle and measurement is essential.

When aligned, the mounts can be glued together using PVA diluted with water, or any strong paper glue, or can simply be attached with masking tape or gummed paper.

HINGE MOUNT

Another type of mount, favoured by art students and anyone carrying a portfolio of works on paper, is the

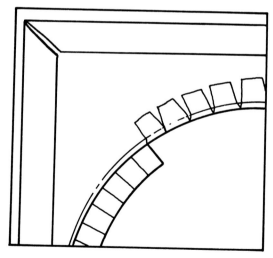

34 When making a fabric mount great care must be taken to ensure the material lies completely flat. Make a diagonal cut on the corner, and cut flaps of fabric on the curve of the window. Fold and glue these onto the reverse side of the mount.

Mount decoration: double mounts (blue and red) and simple line decoration.

hinge mount. This protects the picture from the back and allows the whole picture to be viewed by lifting up the windowed front mount.

Having made a window mount in the normal way, the second step is to cut another piece of card the same size, to serve as a backing board. These two are hinged using masking or linen tape. Finally the picture is taped on to the backing, and is sandwiched safely between the two boards.

METHODS OF MOUNTING

Gummed tape is better for sticking works on paper to the window mount, for this can be readily removed by wetting the tape and peeling it back with no damage to the paper.

If the picture to be mounted is creased or cockled, there is a method of stretching the paper. It will work best with good quality rag or watercolour paper, but should at least help to straighten thinner or inferior paper.

Using gummed strip, fix the picture face down on to a wooden board or table. Make sure that all the sides are firmly taped down. Lightly brush water on the back of the picture and let it dry thoroughly overnight or for some hours. As the paper dries it will become more taut and creases should vanish. I have seen badly creased drawings fixed to a board completely immersed in clean water: when dry they emerge crisp and flat. This does not affect pencil, but should obviously not be tried with other materials that might be affected by water. A little water on the back is sufficient to remove small creases. Artists who use water-based paints on paper use this method to stretch the paper before starting to paint.

All of the mounts so far have been overlapping the edge of the pictures. This is the usual way of mounting, but certain works look better with edges exposed— etchings on good quality paper, or perhaps a miniature

with a painted border that is not quite square. Old paper can also look attractive laid out in this manner, for example old manuscripts with uneven or torn edges. These can be 'tip mounted' on to a complementary backing card. This is done by sticking the picture or paper object to the card using stamp hinges, or small lengths of double-sided tape. For items of value, gummed stamp hinges are preferable for they can easily be removed by applying a little water.

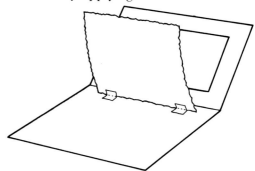

35 *Tip mounting using gummed hinges*

Lastly, an attractive alternative to mount board, and suitable particularly for etchings and other prints, is to use thick watercolour paper. This is made with a variety of texture and is usually a pleasant off-white. The thicker paper will also give a small bevel.

A few hour's practice at measuring, cutting and decorating mounts is all that is needed to start achieving a more professional appearance. With a little imagination you can transform some old photographs or reproductions that you might otherwise have discarded.

Dry mounting

Dry mounting tissue is used for bonding pictures, particularly photographs, to board. The heat is usually applied with a hot press. It can be attempted by the amateur, using a domestic iron, on small items, but it is not advisable for anything large or valuable. It is worth paying a professional to do this for you.

Wet mounting

Reproductions, photographs and prints can be stuck down on to backing board using various glues. There are some good graphic spray glues that are used by paste-up artists. These allow for some readjustment after gluing and are easy to use, if a bit expensive. PVA glue diluted with water is suitable for sticking posters on to board. Probably the cheapest glue is wallpaper adhesive. It is best to glue the back of the picture, and leave it to soak in for a few minutes, before pressing into place. Always start smoothing the picture from the centre moving outwards. It is useful to have a clean dry cloth to rub creases or air bubbles out. If you do not want to glaze posters or prints after having mounted them on to board, they can be protected by applying a few coats of varnish.

5   BASIC SKILLS

There are many types of plain wooden mouldings available, usually either in pine, ash, ramin, oak or mahogany. Pine is the cheapest and softest wood, and the easiest to work with. You should check whether a piece of moulding is straight before buying, particularly if it is made of pine. By holding one end and looking along both edges, you should be able to determine the straightness. These days when speed overrules the tradition of seasoning wood over a period of years, most wood is kiln dried fairly quickly after it is cut down and consequently moves, splits and warps even after it has been milled by the moulding cutters. Though this applies more to the softwoods than the hard ones, it is safer to check all moulding, even if industrially finished, before buying.

It is essential before beginning to make a frame to have one of the devices mentioned in Chapter 3 for cutting a mitre. Not all frames, of course, need to have mitred corners. When using flat timber, butt joins can be used, and for these only a tenon saw is necessary. However, where moulding is required it will be necessary to make mitre joints.

The two mistakes most commonly made in cutting mitres are twisting the moulding whilst cutting, so giving you a sloping instead of a vertical cut; and inaccurate measuring. The first can be avoided by holding the moulding very firmly, or by clamping it with a G clamp (see fig. 38). When using a mitre box, it is a good idea to

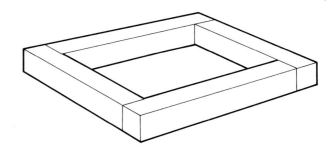

36 *A butt join*

either clamp it to your worktop or sit it into a vice so that it is secure during the sawing of the angles.

If you are too jerky with the saw or your blade is not sharp enough, you are more likely to get an imperfect cut. A steady movement with a sharp saw will give you good mitres.

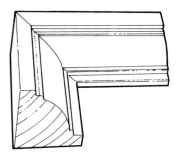

37 *A mitre join*

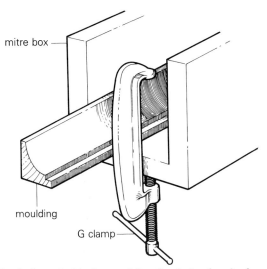

38 *The G clamp holds the moulding firmly in place in the mitre box when cutting*

The second common fault, inaccurate measurement, can only be avoided by concentration and double checking of all measurements at every stage.

When making a square or other rectangular frame, the opposite sides must be identical in size. Any discrepancy will cause openings at the corners and consequently an unstable frame. Small errors of even 2 mm (1/16 in) will be noticeable even to the inexperienced eye, whilst well cut moulding will come together very easily into a frame. For this reason accurate measurement, however tedious it may seem at first, is essential.

MEASURING

The measuring of the mount or picture or article to be framed is very important. Frequently seemingly square corners will not be exactly 90°, so it is essential to make more than one measurement each side to find out whether opposite sides are equal. If they are only fractionally out, this can be lost behind the rebate of the moulding. However, if it is a significant amount, either

some measure must be shaved off the picture or some amount must be covered using a slip frame or some other device. This will be discussed later.

A simple approximate method of measuring is started by looking at the rebate.

All picture frame moulding is made with a rebate, except for slip moulding and beading.

The size of the rebate differs slightly, the thinner mouldings may have 4 mm (1/8 in) and the wider ones up to 1 cm (1/2 in) or more. On most of the middle range moulding sizes, the rebate is generally 5 mm (1/4 in). Before buying moulding it is wise to check the size of the rebate to see how much of your picture or object will be hidden.

If we subtract the rebate size from the picture size and measure from the inside edge, along the moulding, marking off the dimension on the rebate, we would get such a tight fit that it would be necessary to trim the picture. In order to get a comfortable but not loose fit, we can divide the rebate in half and subtract that amount. This will allow 2–4 mm (1/16–1/8 in) extra space depending on the size of the rebate.

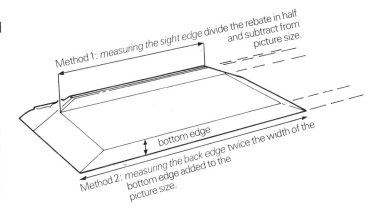

39 *Measuring the picture frame moulding*

This of course is not the only way to measure; some people prefer to measure the outer edge and mark on the back of the frame. For this procedure, twice the bottom edge of the moulding is added to the picture measurements, plus 2 mm (1/16 in) to allow for a comfortable fit. Another method is to allow twice the width, plus 2.5 cm (1 in) extra, and then cut your moulding to this larger size. By holding the picture to the inside of the rebate you can mark off the size easily and trim off the extra amount.

It is possible after the first side is cut to hold the moulding back to back with the uncut length and mark off the measure on the second side without a ruler. But beginners should practise their measuring as much. as possible and since measuring with a ruler takes only a few seconds more, it is safer to measure each of the sides individually. Later after some practice these shortcuts can be used.

Trimming the moulding may be difficult in a simple mitre box, and is much easier with a mitre saw or morso cutter. However, if you hold your moulding firmly and cut slowly and evenly, it should be possible to trim off a few millimetres. This is obviously made easier if your tenon saw blade is thin and sharp. More experienced carpenters could try shaving off minute discrepancies with a very sharp chisel, but this takes some practice. Often the simple way out is to shorten both sides by measuring and re-cutting, but if you are working to a fixed size it will be necessary to cut another piece of moulding. Bench trimmers can be bought from good tool shops and are very useful, but out of the price range of most beginners. Finally, with careful concentration, it should not be necessary to trim.

ASSEMBLING THE FRAME

Assuming that we now have four pieces of moulding, with opposite sides exactly the same size, we can proceed to the next step, which is the assembly using nails and glue. It is possible to use a vice for this purpose, as described in Chapter 3; however, you will need plenty of practice and an electric drill. There are various types of corner cramps on the market (see pages 40–41). If you have four corner cramps—or the Elwood wire cramp or similar machine—you can join all four sides in one procedure. Set the frame out first in clamps without using glue so that you can check the assembly of the frame, and that the corners are accurate before you glue. Then it is just a matter of taking out two opposite sides in sequence, gluing both ends, and replacing them in the cramps; adjust the screws for final tightness, and wipe off excess glue with a damp cloth.

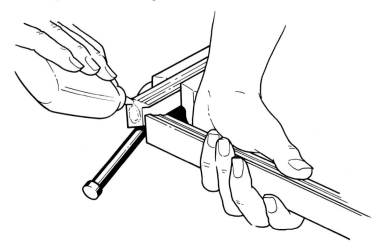

40 *Joining a corner in a vice*

If you have only two cramps, or you are using a vice, you will need to make two L-shaped sections first, and then join these together in your final assembly. Be sure that you join the right sides together or you will end up with a very strange shape.

If you have an electric drill, it is possible to drill and

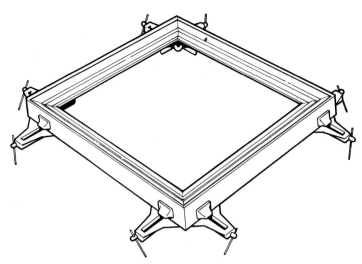

41 Joining a frame with four corner cramps

A selection of finished frames.

nail whilst the glue is setting; but with hardwoods this is not advisable. In general, unless you are in a hurry, it is safer to allow the glue to harden and set before nailing.

For the beginner who wishes to improvise, rather than buy tools, it is possible to assemble a frame using strong string or cord for the tension. An alternative is thin cable, or long rubber strips. These can be made very cheaply and used to good effect. For the final tightening, wedges should be inserted around all sides of the frame.

A useful tool in all the assembly procedures is the 90° square or Trisquare. These sometimes come with a 45° ridge as well. Using the square you can check all your corners and adjust where necessary. Often too much tension will result in the frame distorting.

When you are satisfied that the glue has set, drill your pilot holes ready for nailing. A bradawl will be sufficient for softwoods, but a small hand drill is useful for the harder woods. Some framers prefer to nail only into the top or bottom of the frame so that there are no marks on the visible sides of the frame. This is quite a good idea, but if you punch your nails slightly below the surface of the wood and use wood-filler they should be nearly invisible. Two nails per corner are normal, but on the thinner mouldings one is usually sufficient.

There are many types of nails available, and it is much better to use the right type and size of nail to avoid splitting or damaging the wood. With a good pair of pliers most nails can be trimmed to a suitable size.

CUTTING GLASS

Cutting glass looks more difficult than it actually is. Great care, though, must be exercised when handling the glass. Sharp edges can cut deeply into the fingers with very little pressure.

A flat, preferably large, surface is essential for cutting glass. A blanket or sheets of newspaper will pad your workbench or table sufficiently. Ensure that there are no bumps, protrusions or grit anywhere underneath the glass, for this may well cause the glass to break in the wrong place whilst cutting. A metal straight edge, or even better a T-square, are necessary for supporting the cutter as you draw it along the glass.

Whichever type of glass cutter you are using (see page 42), it will need to be lubricated before scoring the glass. One can buy special thin cutting oil or else use methylated spirits. A recent useful innovation is a cutter that looks like a pen and holds its own cutting oil like ink in a barrel in the stem. Thus as you cut the wheel is lubricated from above. A more expensive cutter will have replaceable heads and is therefore better, because it is essential to have a sharp wheel to avoid badly scored lines and incorrect breaks in the glass.

The most widely used glass for framing is 2 mm (1/16 in) clear glass. 3 mm (1/8 in) glass is normally used for windows, but can be used in frames—though large areas will be heavy. Non-reflective glass is often used nowadays for prints and watercolours; this is nearly double the price, but is very popular.

Before cutting large expensive pieces of glass, it is wiser to practise on small offcuts you may have lying around the house. It is much easier to cut thin glass, so it is advisable to practise on this.

A felt or fibre-tip pen will mark the glass clearly enough for you to see whilst cutting. Position the glass on the bench and line up the straight edge a little away from your marks to allow for the width of the glass cutting head. Keeping a firm, even pressure downwards, pull the glass cutter towards you. Hold the cutter like a pencil and keep it fairly upright so that there is unrestricted contact between the cutting wheel and the glass. As you score along the glass it should make a hissing sound. The scored line will be visible. It is only necessary to score once; in fact, a second attempt on the same line will probably result in breaking the glass and damaging your cutter.

The scored line can be tapped all the way along using the knob usually positioned at the end of the stem of the glass cutter. You may tap fairly vigorously, particularly on thick glass or curved lines, as this makes the breaking more even later on. On normal straight cuts on thin glass it is not usually necessary to tap the glass.

To break the glass along the scored line, simply position the glass on the edge of the table or edge of the ruler with the scored line along the breaking edge and apply pressure to both sides of the line. The glass, properly scored, will break evenly. If necessary, for clip frames, etc., the edges of the glass can be smoothed with glass paper.

For cutting small amounts of glass off a large piece it is necessary to have special glass-breaking pliers (see fig 42). These have wide grips that can break off long pieces of thin glass. Position the glass on the edge of a table, hold the pliers so that the grips are along the scored line, and break the glass downwards. Using ordinary pliers it is very easy to break the entire sheet of glass when trying to pull small pieces off.

For curves and ovals, a template of cardboard is useful as a guide for the cutter. For circles, compasses with a cutting head can be bought or improvised. These take more practice and need to have each section of the curve broken as you progress around the shape.

FINAL ASSEMBLY

By this stage, we should have our frame assembled, glued, pinned and finished with sandpaper, wood-filler, etc. It is usually easier to complete the frame—with stain, paint, lacquer, varnish or whichever finish is required—before the final assembly. Small adjustments

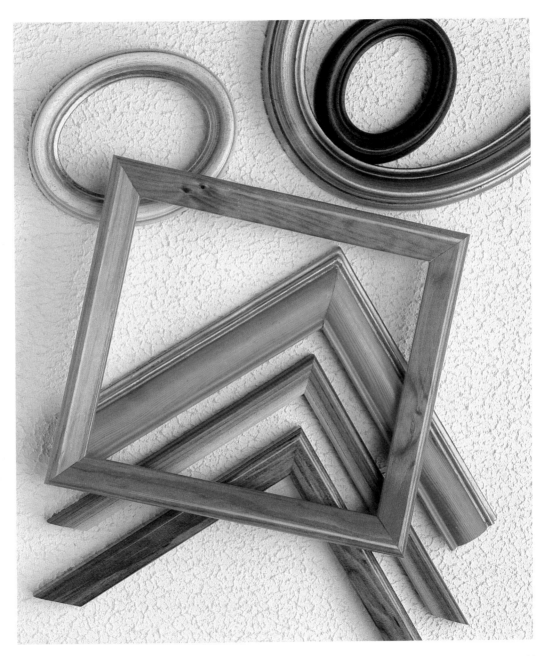

Wooden frames can be stained, lacquered and gilded for a variety of finishes.

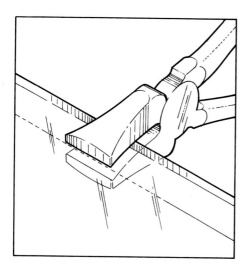

42 Using glass-breaking pliers to break off small pieces of glass

and waxing can be done afterwards, but there is always a risk of damaging the glass and picture.

Glass, mount and backing board should all be the same size and fit snugly into the rebate of the frame. If there is any significant movement inside the frame it is advisable to stick the moving parts to the frame with Sellotape or to wedge them with small pieces of wood. You will find that when you make your final attachments at the back, any movement will cause the mount to shift out of alignment with the frame.

The backing board most commonly used is 3 mm (⅛ in) hardboard. This is cheap and durable and more rigid than cardboard. It can be cut by scoring three or four times with a craft knife and then breaking, like glass, over the edge of a workbench or table top. Alternatively, it can be sawn. Less durable, but lighter and easier to cut, is backing board made of card. This can be found in most graphic or artists' supply shops.

If you use triangular hangers or D rings, diagonal cuts a few centimetres towards the centre of the board and again a third of the way down from the top need to be cut into the backing board (cardboard is not strong enough for these fastenings). This can be done with a craft knife. The fastenings are then fed through the cuts and the rings left exposed at the back. The flanges on the inside of the backing board are then opened, hammered flat, and usually covered with masking tape to prevent contact with the picture.

The glass can be cleaned with a brand spray, or a cheaper alternative is methylated spirits mixed with water.

Place the frame face downwards on the working surface. Next the glass, clean and dust-free, is inserted; then the picture with or without a mount; and lastly the backing board. At this stage it is advisable to turn the whole package over carefully and to check that it is all in alignment and that there is no dust between the picture and glass.

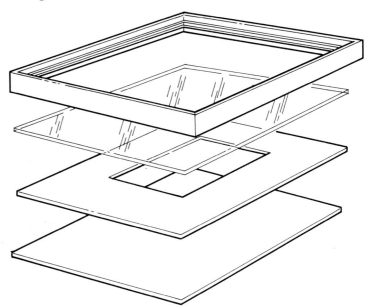

43 Final assembly

Alternatively, lay the backing board down first, then the picture and mount, and then the glass. In this way you can check for dust as you are assembling. Lastly, the frame is placed over the rest and turned over.

If you have a glazing gun, small diamond arrows can be fixed into the back of the frame taking care to support the side that you are driving into by a wall or piece of timber. Otherwise, nail with small tacks (brads) or pins every few centimetres—making a small pilot hole first.

Lastly, gummed paper tape is stuck down over the join between frame and backing board. This forms a barrier against dust and dirt and makes the whole appearance of the back more neat and tidy.

The framed picture is now complete and ready for the fastenings. There are a number of different types available (discussed in Chapter 3). With the aid of a bradawl, hooks can be screwed into the back of the frame, usually about a third of the way down from the top. Strong cord or brass wire can then be attached; pull this taut if you do not want the cord to be visible.

The framed picture is now complete and should be a strong and durable surround as well as enhancing the picture or object. For the professional touch, the back should be as neat as the front, there should not be any dust or marks on the picture or mount, and the picture, mount and frame should be in alignment.

6 FINISHES

There are an enormous range of finished mouldings available from picture-frame moulding suppliers. Many are imported from Italy, Holland and further away places such as Taiwan and Korea. A lot of these are industrially gilded and ornamented in a large variety of thickness and composition. Few are copies of period pieces, but they are still attractive and useful for certain paintings. There are plainer mouldings that are also industrially gilded and sprayed with a range of coloured varnishes. These have very smooth, perfect finishes and great care is needed when cutting them, as damage to the surface is often tricky to repair. You may find a finished moulding that complements your picture or your home or hopefully both, but they are fairly expensive and do not have quite the same satisfaction as finishing your own frame. The finish is often the most rewarding and enjoyable part of the whole job.

WOOD STAINING

The majority of plain wood mouldings are either pine or ramin (a hardwood). These are both quite pale and are often enhanced by adding a wood stain. The more expensive hardwood mouldings such as oak and mahogany are improved with a light stain. This emphasizes the natural qualities of the timber and the attractive figuring in the grain.

It is much easier to stain the wood along the length of the moulding before cutting. This avoids the difficulty of trying to paint the stain evenly around the corners of the frame. It also avoids the kind of spotting that can result from invisible residue of glue and grease resisting the stain.

For better results on plain wooden mouldings rub down with medium and then fine sandpaper to get a very smooth surface. Dampen a cloth lightly with white spirit and wipe clean the outside surfaces of the moulding. This will enable the wood to absorb the stain more easily.

The stain can then be applied either with a brush or rubbed into the wood using fine steel wool (000 grade). It is advisable to use rubber gloves during this process, as wood stains are difficult to remove from hands. When dry the stain can be cut back in colour by rubbing with steel wool, or reduced further with white spirit. Good quality furniture wax (usually incorporating beeswax) will finish a wood stain very nicely. For a harder gloss finish shellac or varnishes can be applied. On the harder woods a little linseed oil can be rubbed into the wood using a soft cloth—this deepens the colour and enriches the wood. Later the mouldings can be waxed or varnished.

French polishing can really only be learnt successfully through practical teaching. There are, however, quick drying shellacs that can be used by the amateur, and these are alcohol based. They are thinned, and the brushes cleaned in methylated spirits. One can add earth colours (umber, sienna, ochre) to shellac and paint it on as a stain.

A selection of mounts, miniatures and finished frames displaying the choice and variety open to the frame-maker.

It is important to allow each coat of shellac to dry between coats, for rucking in the texture occurs easily, if applying a new coat on top of shellac that is still tacky. A fluent action with a wide brush, sweeping along the moulding, with as few strokes as possible, will give the smoothest surface. If dribbles and rucking occur, wait until the surface is dry, and then cut back with steel wool or fine sandpaper before repainting. These shellac stains can be painted over the spirit stains mentioned earlier to achieve the richness of a glaze.

The spirit stains may be mixed together to achieve more varied tones, or one may be applied on top of another—allowing a suitable time for drying. On no account, though, should spirit stains be added to shellac; the result is disastrous.

PAINTING

You can achieve very successful finishes using commercially produced paints: vinyl emulsions, acrylic, enamel paints or oil-based gloss or silk finish paints. It is always good policy to have an even surface on which to paint. A few coats of undercoat lightly rubbed with fine sandpaper will give you an excellent ground for most paints.

An alternative which is cheaper if you want to mix a large quantity of paint, are paints that can be made from pigment. Pigments (powder colour) vary in quality and price from the artist quality to the coarser varieties. A good range of earth colours (umber, sienna, ochre and black) are available at cheap prices from french polish suppliers. These colours can be suspended in shellac or mixed with PVA glue and water to get different finishes. Shellac dries quite quickly and so is useful as a medium for decorating frames. The PVA mix will give a poster colour quality to the pigment and a matt finish on the frame. Pigment can also be suspended in water alone, but for this kind of watercolour wash you really need a gesso ground.

GESSO

Gesso, literally the Italian for plaster, has been used for centuries as a ground for painting and gilding. It is a little time consuming to prepare, but is very cheap to make and provides an excellent surface for a variety of finishes.

For frames and panel painting, gesso can be made in the following manner. Rabbit skin or parchment glue needs to be soaked overnight in cold water. These glues are either in sheet or pearl form and when dry can be kept almost indefinitely. When they have been soaked, they can be kept in cool conditions for a few days only; in a fridge they will last a bit longer.

Take some of this soaked glue and weigh it. Add 9 parts water to 1 part glue and place in a double boiler (or in a tin can inside a saucepan of water). This needs to be gently heated until the glue has melted. Pour a little of this mixture into another jar or tin. This can later be thinned with more water and used as a thin size coat over the wood and gesso.

To the mixture add refined gilder's whiting. Coarser whiting may be more available; this needs to be carefully sieved before adding to the glue. Enough whiting should be added to make the mixture into a smooth creamy texture. If the gesso is still lumpy it may need to be sieved through a muslin cloth. Great care must be taken not to overheat the gesso; the glue is easily destroyed by heat and the gesso will then be useless and, if applied, will crack and crumble when dry. A few small drops of glycerine can be added to soften the texture. Professional gilders often mix their gesso the day before they use it. When cool the gesso sets into a white jelly. This jelly can be tested for strength by pushing a finger into it. If the mixture offers too much resistance, it should be thinned with a little more water. If the mixture is too loose and has hardly set at all, more glue should be added. Ideally the gesso should be a firm jelly that the finger can penetrate easily.

Brush over the wood with a little of the thinned size coat. This must be allowed to dry thoroughly. The gesso is then applied warm on to the wood. It is much better to paint a large number of thin coats than a few thick coats. There are no shortcuts in the preparation and application of gesso. Some framers like to paint the gesso in different directions with each coat, so giving the texture more strength. It is not necessary to wait for each coat to dry thoroughly before applying the next, but a few minutes is advisable. Five or six coats is enough for most frames, but where an etched pattern in the gesso is required a few more coats will allow a deeper etch. Powder colour (pigment) can be added to the gesso to get some very attractive finishes. When dry, the gesso can be rubbed down with garnet paper and waxed or varnished. Pigment should be very thoroughly mixed with the gesso, or else a variation of tone and streaks will appear. Artists often like to tint their ground in this way prior to painting.

After the last coat of gesso is applied it is essential to wait for a few hours to allow the gesso to dry thoroughly. Wet and dry garnet paper is used to rub down. This paper can be used wet to smooth the gesso, the residue of water can be wiped off with cotton wool, and in this manner you can achieve a smooth marble-like surface. Be careful not to use too much water, for if you do you will wipe off too much gesso and expose the wood. Where only a few coats of gesso are used, better results will be achieved if you use fine sandpaper or garnet paper without water.

When the gesso is completely smooth, the previously mixed thin size can be painted over it. This renders the gesso less absorbent so that colour laid on top will not sink into it. There is now a synthetic acrylic-based gesso that can be applied cold and is already mixed. It may be less trouble but is quite expensive—and must not be used for gilding.

LACQUERWORK

Being so smooth, the gesso surface is ideal for lacquerwork. Colour can be added to shellac for this purpose. Exact quantities are hard to define, but too much pigment in shellac will result in a matt grainy texture (which will need to be rubbed down), and too little will mean that a large number of coats will be needed to achieve the desired tone. You will need to use as many coats as will make the colour even around the frame. Four or five should be sufficient. Allow the surface to dry thoroughly before cutting back with fine garnet paper. A coat of transparent shellac can be added for the finish, or for a more durable surface some glaze varnish or ormolu lacquer can be used. It is very helpful when trying to get a very smooth surface to have a soft wide brush with which to paint, and to lay the colour on in smooth fluent strokes, allowing the colour to dry between coats.

As an alternative to shellac and colour, gouache or simply pigment in a very thin size solution goes on to a gesso surface very well. Again it is difficult to control the even spread of colour, and it is made easier by having to hand large, flat, soft brushes to control the washes. Very attractive transparent washes can be applied in this manner. Where there is some texture on the gesso, or etched pattern, or simple grooves and recesses on the moulding, a very attractive result can be obtained by brushing colour on and then rubbing it out with a slightly damp sponge. This leaves a residue of colour collecting in the pattern and recesses of the frame. These colour washes can be protected and deepened in colour by a finish in either wax or varnish.

ETCHED PATTERNS

The early Renaissance frames, often called Florentine, were distinctive for their wide flat central borders of painted, etched or embossed ornament with moulding either side. Some are simple, others much more elaborate. There are some very good examples in the National Gallery, London. These patterns are usually painted with a very free hand, and have an ease and grace to them that an adherence to a too rigid form of exact patterning would lose.

Patterns can be drawn or traced on to gesso and then etched, using a bradawl or nail. The thicker the gesso the deeper you are able to etch. These marks can later be picked out in colour or in a gold finish.

METALLIC WAXES

Waxes can give a very good gold, silver, pewter or copper effect, and are particularly pleasing on a gesso surface. The gesso allows the wax to be burnished, thus imitating quite well the burnish of true gilding—though obviously not so bright.

These waxes are readily available in different forms from most art shops. The more expensive variety (Treasure gold) is generally thought the best. However, it is much cheaper to fashion your own using a mixture of beeswax and canauba wax melted in turpentine and mixed with bronze powders of your choice. Wax media can also be bought from shops ready mixed. This is a comparatively simple procedure; the wax should not be heated too fiercely, and a double boiler or tin in a saucepan is the best method. The metallic wax should be stored in an airtight container to preserve it.

Rather than apply these metallic waxes straight on to a gesso ground, it is more pleasing to use a colour underneath. This will make it resemble a gilded finish more closely. For this, 'bole' such as is used for gilding or gouache can be employed. The bole, which comes in a variety of colours, is normally added to a thin rabbit size solution and painted on warm. It must be allowed to dry completely between each coat. Two coats should be enough. When dry, this can be rubbed with a soft cloth before applying the wax. Gouache should only need one coat and can also be smoothed with a cloth. These colours will allow the wax to be burnished, whilst shellac, acrylic or oil-based colour will prevent this.

For a bright gold finish, an ochre or yellow-orange undercoat enhances the gold. For a more antique look, a terracotta colour with perhaps some black added will give maturity to the gold. Silver and pewter waxes look very well with blue or black underneath. Here there is plenty of room for experiment; green also looks rich under gold, and grey under silver.

The wax should be allowed to harden for a few hours before polishing with a soft cloth, and left for a few days before burnishing with a gilder's agate stone. These burnishers come in a wide variety of size and shape and are very smooth semi-precious agates mounted on a wooden handle. Over a smooth flat surface it is best to manipulate them always in the same direction. It is wise to burnish lightly at first to test the strength of your gesso. Vigorous burnishing can cause weak gesso to crack and chip.

For a distressed, antique look, it is sometimes easier not to apply the metallic wax all over the frame but to allow recesses to be covered only in their undercoat colour, leaving the gold to touch highlights. However the waxes can be distressed, using fine steel wool (000 grade) and a little turpentine. Take care to distress evenly all over the frame to achieve a uniformity of colour.

STAINING WAXES

For subtle effects of tone, on painted or stained frames, pigments can be added to furniture wax and applied over the paint or stain. Special staining waxes can be bought from french polishing suppliers with colour already added. However, for more flexibility pigments can be mixed into clear wax.

A very bright geranium red frame, for example, may be too loud a colour on its own, but with a little black wax rubbed in, it becomes softer whilst still retaining its richness. Similarly, on a light oak stain some umber colour added to wax and polished on top will give an antique maturity to the wood. These waxes are very useful for toning down, but cannot change a colour radically. Ordinary furniture wax may be used, preferably containing some beeswax.

FAUX MARBRE

For colour mixes and *trompe l'oeil* effects, there are various 'scumble glazes' that can be bought. Some have colour added, others are transparent. These are media that allow the colour to remain wet and pliable for a long period of time, usually a few hours. When using these scumbles it is advisable to have linseed oil and turpentine to hand to thin the mixtures. If you are trying to achieve a marble or wood grain finish, it is important to have the right surface appearance. Gesso is a very good ground for a marble sheen. If the scumbles have texture they will rob the surface of this smooth look. A number of implements such as feathers, sponges and combs as well as brushes are useful. For realistic marble and wood grain it is very helpful to have a sample of material from which to copy.

It is common practice to have a base colour as an undercoat. For an oak wood grain, for example, an ochre undercoat may be used. This has transparent shellac painted over the top to protect it from the scumble and to allow you to rub out the top colours without interfering with the base coat. Similarly, for a Sicilian marble finish a very pale grey undercoat may be used, and darker and lighter veining superimposed.

Rubber or special thin metal combs can be used to imitate wood grain. The surface should then be stippled over with a hog brush so that the colour and texture can be flattened a little. For marble and precious stone effects, feathers are sometimes used to coax the fluid paint into veins and patterns. Allowing the oil and spirits to mingle freely, with the minimum of brushwork, often gives you the best results. Dribbling or splattering colour on to another wet colour by tapping your brush against a wooden block is another method of decoration.

7 CARE AND RESTORATION

People often come across, or are given, old frames of all kinds that are attractive but in need of attention. Many are severely damaged, whilst others only need cleaning and a minimum amount of repair.

An important factor to bear in mind, when contemplating the restoration of a frame, is the amount of time involved in the process. For some frames, sadly, restoration is not worthwhile. They should be left alone, or used for the wooden base rather than have weeks of work, trying to make something of very little, wasted on them.

WOOD FRAMES

Old wood frames, plain or carved, can often be cleaned with a wax or varnish remover such as acetone or white spirit. The wood graining in old frames is frequently very beautiful and only needs a little linseed oil to deepen the colour and give life to the dry wood. The glue in the mitres will often have perished, and the corners will need tightening. Pliers and metal clips are excellent for this purpose. Pull the corners a little apart, pour glue into them, helping it into the mitre with a thin blade. Close the corners with the metal clips or one of the other suitable cramps and wipe off the excess glue with a damp cloth before it sets. Sometimes this is not enough and the frame needs to be pulled apart completely, the nails extracted, and perhaps the mitres re-cut. Take care to extract all the nails before before re-cutting the mitres.

If there are any traces of woodworm or rot, it is a good

A flat, gilded frame in a bad state of repair.

idea to treat the wood with one of the proprietary brands of wood preservative; take care to find a transparent one.

Where a french polish or lacquer finish has been used

The frame has been re-gessoed, and has been given an undercoat of red bole. Gold wax has been applied, polished and burnished. The glass has been replaced and the print cleaned.

on a frame and there are marks and scratches, some retouching with shellac and matching pigment will often be sufficient.

Carved wood frames are now quite rare and highly sought after by antique dealers. If you have one in need of repair, it would be wiser to consult a woodcarver rather than attempting a repair yourself.

ANTIQUE MOULDED FRAMES

There are very many of these nineteenth-century composition frames still in existence. Usually they have been gilded at least in part. They often do require a long time to restore well. Until recently they were considered to be largely worthless, particularly if damaged, and a very poor relation to the carved gilded frame.

Some people used to immerse whole frames in water to destroy all the composition and retain the wooden frames for a more contemporary appearance. There is now a renewed appreciation of the skill and ingenuity that went into the construction and decoration of these frames. The composition of the moulded pattern tends to dry and crack with age and so falls away from the wood eventually. If this is the case all over the frame, it is a major task to restore and it may be better to drop the project unless the frame is of importance or an unusual pattern. Where only a few ornaments are missing they can be recast from the existing ones. A very useful substance for smaller pieces is a moulding compound in powder form, much the same as that used by dentists for taking impressions of teeth. It sets very quickly when water is added, so speed in mixing and applying is essential. A little oil or Vaseline as a resist can be brushed over the ornament to be moulded; the compound is then packed on top and left until set. Later, either dental or other hard plaster can be used as a filler for the mould. After thirty minutes or so the moulded piece should be dry enough to separate from the mould, be cleaned with

Recasting by applying a silicone rubber mould.

a small knife and glued into place. Unfortunately moulding compounds do not last (being based on an organic seaweed substance). In a plastic bag, in the fridge, the mould might last a couple of weeks, but exposed to the air, only a couple of days. For larger ornaments and more durable moulds it will be necessary to use silicone rubber, or fibre glass. These compositions are available from specialist moulding shops. The silicone rubber process is more time-consuming, for the mix takes longer to dry. However, it gives high definition and is very durable.

Plaster impressions can then be made from the rubber mould.

If you are repairing a gilded ornamented frame, it is best to clean the frame carefully first so that you can see all the faults and can match the gold colour. Acetone is a good cleaner of most gilded surfaces, though care must be taken not to wipe off the delicate gold leaf as well as the dirt. Small cracks in the frame can be filled either with a fine surface filler or some other smooth strong filler.

When all the moulded parts are in place, they should be lightly covered in gesso, so that the pattern is not obscured, and then coloured to match the bole of the original.

On bright water-gilded frames it may be necessary to use real gold leaf. This can either be glued on, using special gold size, or water-gilded. If, however, the original gold is not too bright, it is easier and more effective to restore with gold wax on top of bole colour and gesso. This can be burnished and distressed to match the antique sheen. Where water gilding has been used, this can be distressed for an antique appearance with a soft cloth and beeswax. For glued gold, a light wash or a stained wax can tone down the brightness.

LACQUER FRAMES

These frames, usually nineteenth century, are generally black with a thin decorated gold beading or slip. They are wooden frames coated in gesso and ebonized with black lacquer. Over the years these perfect surfaces are liable to chip and crack and become scratched. If the gesso surface is still intact, it can be rubbed down with steel wool (000 grade) or fine sandpaper and then filled with gesso or a fine filler. Before painting it must be rubbed down until there is a fine smooth surface. Shellac, mixed with black or a matching colour, can then be applied. Two or three coats should be enough. Leave this to dry and then cut back with fine garnet paper. Some lacquer or transparent glaze will protect the surface. For extra shine, two or three coats of lacquer can be applied and cut back in between coats.

If the gesso is loose in large areas it will need to be soaked off and then repainted with gesso. This will take a long time and will probably not be worth doing unless it is a particularly handsome frame.

It is not possible to deal with all types of restoration in this small book. However, with a little knowledge of fillers and finishes, some ingenuity and hard work, it is possible to restore most old frames.

The finished frame with all the corners replaced. The frame has been cleaned and covered with gesso where necessary. A coat of bole has been applied over the whole frame, and then a wax gold finish.

74

SELECTED FRAMES ON VIEW
TO THE PUBLIC

The Rucellai Madonna by Duccio, 1285 (Church of Santa Maria Novella, Florence). Plain shape, painted with medallions of saints and prophets.

The Coronation of the Virgin, 1394 (Metropolitan Museum of Art, New York). Florentine altar-piece, a triptych which is shaped like a cross-section of the church. Both picture and frame have a gold ground and are painted in tempera. The predella is large and has pictures painted on it, an idea which Rossetti was to use in the nineteenth century for several of his Pre-Raphaelite paintings.

Virgin and Child with Saints by Duccio, early fourteenth century (National Gallery, London). Another altar-piece.

Adoration of the Magi by Gentile da Fabriano, 1423 (Uffizi Gallery, Florence). A very ornate frame, gilded and painted, but allowing the altar-piece to become one whole painting instead of a triptych.

Madonna and Child with Saints by Andrea di Vanni, *c.* 1400 (Santo Stefano, Siena). An example of a Siennese altar-piece.

Altar of St Clare, School of Cologne, mid-fourteenth century (Cologne Cathedral). Ornate German carved altar-piece; the hinged wings of the triptych are painted on the back with the same architectural details of the frame that are carved on the front, both in small detailed decoration.

John the Evangelist, and *St Mary Magdalene*, by Stefan Lochner, before 1415 (Museum Boymans-van Beunigen, Rotterdam). Examples of northern European panel paintings carved in one piece, quite plain but painted with a delicate pattern around the frame.

St Luke Painting the Virgin by a Follower of Quentin Massys, first half of sixteenth century (National Gallery, London). Altar-piece wing with a painting of an artist at work on a panel with the frame ready carved out of it.

The Goldsmith Jan de Leeuwe by Jan van Eyck, 1436 (Kunsthistorisches Museum, Vienna). A Flemish frame which was probably painted by the artist, with an inscription right round it giving details of the subject of the portrait.

Margaret van Eyck by Jan van Eyck, 1439 (Groenige Museum, Bruges).

Man in a Turban by Jan van Eyck (National Gallery, London).

Madonna and Child with Saints and Crucifixion by School of Paris (known as the Large Bargello Diptych), *c.* 1390 (Museo Nazionale, Florence). A simple overall shape reveals beautifully carved detail inside the two panels when they are opened.

Madonna and Child by Paris Bordone, sixteenth century (Rijksmuseum, Amsterdam). An Italian frame which is completely free of architectural elements; a plainly shaped, moulded frame using three main bands of ornament.

Madonna and Child by Cima da Conegliano, *c.* 1500 (Rijksmuseum, Amsterdam). This frame is another sixteenth-century Italian example.

Madonna and Child with Saints by Francesco Bissolo, sixteenth century (Rijksmuseum, Amsterdam). Another variation on the three bands of ornament.

James I by Mytens, 1620 (Knole, Kent). A fairly ornate frame, carved, painted and gilded.

Infanta Margareta Theresa from the Workshop of Velasquez, *c.* 1664 (Kunsthistorisches Museum, Vienna). A Spanish frame showing the influence of Italian Renaissance frames combined with the Spanish craftsman's feel for the wood itself. The gold leaf is a duller, deeper tone of brownish gold.

Hélène Fourment by Peter Paul Rubens, *c.* 1630–31 (Rijksmuseum, Amsterdam). A French frame of the Louis XIV period, when France had overtaken Italy in becoming the centre of influence.

Adoration of the Golden Calf by Nicolas Poussin, *c.* 1635–7 (National Gallery, London). A late Louis XIV frame, showing the clear delicate carving which is made possible by the technique of re-cutting the thick gesso surface before gilding.

The Rape of the Sabines by Nicolas Poussin (Metropolitan Museum of Art, New York).

Galerie des Glaces, 1684 (Versailles). This great room, which fired the imagination of all Europe, was created by Jules-Hardouin Mansart for Louis XIV. It has seventeen tall arched windows opposite their respective mirrors which are framed with gilt bronze mouldings. This gives us an idea of the lavishness of décor with which pictures and frames had to relate.

The Doctor's Visit by Samuel van Hoogstraten (Rijksmuseum, Amsterdam). This is a Dutch frame in the Louis XIII style, most of which seem to have been made for export rather than used in Dutch households.

William I of Orange by Thomas de Key, second half of sixteenth century (Rijksmuseum, Amsterdam). An example of a Dutch border frame, derived from the late Renaissance Italian moulding frames.

The Guitar Player by Johannes Vermeer, seventeenth century (Kenwood, Hampstead Heath, London).

Henry VII, fifteenth century (National Portrait Gallery, London). An English frame, fairly plain, carved out of the panel.

Henry VIII, 1520 (National Portrait Gallery, London). Painted and grained.

Madonna and Child with Saints and Donors by Filippino Lippi, ?1486 (Santo Spirito, Florence). A typical Florentine altar-piece of the early Renaissance, based on classical architecture.

Altar of St Mark by Bartolommeo Vivarini, 1474 (Church of the Frari, Venice). Still very much influenced by Gothic architecture.

Madonna and Child with Saints by Bartolommeo Vivarini, 1482 (Church of the Frari, Venice). Another altar-piece in the same church made by him six years later, which is also a triptych but influenced by Renaissance architecture.

Madonna and Child with Saints by Giovanni Bellini, 1488 (Church of the Frari, Venice). Frame by Jacopo da Faenza; a more ornate Renaissance style.

Portrait of a Girl from the Studio of Domenico Ghirlandaio, fifteenth century (National Gallery, London). An early Italian Renaissance frame for a portrait.

Madonna and Child by Luca della Robbia, 1455 (Museo Nazionale, Florence). A glazed terracotta tondo; one of the medallions from Tuscany that inspired the tondo frames popular with the great Renaissance painters.

Holy Family by Michelangelo Buonarroti, 1504 (Uffizi Gallery, Florence). Frame made by Antonio Barile; a tondo frame of the Renaissance designed with great originality and exquisitely carved. Barile was from Siena.

Madonna and Child by Raphael, 1505 (Kunsthistorisches Museum, Vienna).

Madonna and Child by Master of San Miniato, *c.* 1470 (Rijksmuseum, Amsterdam). Frame still linked to architecture.

Portrait of a Woman by Ambrogio de Predis, late fifteenth or early sixteenth century (Rijksmuseum, Amsterdam). Similar to the above.

Madonna and Child by Giorgio Schiavone, late fifteenth century (Rijksmuseum, Amsterdam). Paintings were sometimes set into the wall, like this one, and often were given very simple frames.

The Adoration of the Holy Trinity by Albrecht Dürer, 1511 (Germanisches Nationalmuseum, Nürnberg). An example of the influence of the Italian Renaissance on German frames: a highly ornate frame designed by the artist and probably made by Veit Stoss, who has altered the original design slightly, to its detriment.

The Letter by Johannes Vermeer, 1660 (Rijksmuseum, Amsterdam). A distinctive Dutch frame in dark wood, wide and plain with rippled mouldings. This one is made of ebony, and holds the picture out towards the viewer.

The Eve of St Nicholas by Jan Steen, 1660–65 (Rijksmuseum, Amsterdam). This is an example of a frame in the Lutma style, carved with naturalistic fruit and flowers in quite high relief, but giving an overall feeling of flatness and broadness. This frame has a cherub's head at the top centre.

Self Portrait by Ferdinand Bol, seventeenth century (Rijksmuseum, Amsterdam). This frame is attributed to Johan Lutma himself. It is surmounted by a sunflower, symbol of the art of painting, and its thin inner moulding is more obvious than that of the one above.

Portrait of a Naval Officer, c. 1675 (Rijksmuseum, Amsterdam). This Lutma style frame uses the trappings of war as its motifs for decoration and is surmounted by a crest. It was common to use clusters of ornament to accentuate the centre of each side of the frame in this way.

Charles II and *Aubrey de Vere*, 1670 (Dulwich Picture Gallery). A pair of examples of the *genre auriculaire* frame, carved and gilt with flattish auricular scrolls.

Philip IV of Spain by the Studio of Velasquez, late seventeenth century (Dulwich Picture Gallery).

Two Peasant Boys by Murillo, late seventeenth century (Dulwich Picture Gallery).

The Virgin of the Immaculate Conception by Juan de Valdes-Leal, seventeenth century (Courtauld Institute Galleries). Another Spanish frame with deep carving, quite elaborate.

The Music Lesson by Nicolas Lancret, 1743 (Musée du Louvre, Paris). French frames became more and more ornate, and this is an example of a rococo frame, with not a straight line to be seen.

Grinling Gibbons frame (Victoria and Albert Museum, London). This frame was made for a painting, although mirror frames were in the same vein. The inner rectangle is quite plain, but the naturalistic garlands of fruit, flowers, foliage and seashells hang in profusion over the outer edges.

English mirror frame, 1730/40 (Victoria and Albert Museum, London: W.86–1911). Probably designed by William Kent for Frederick Prince of Wales and made by Benjamin Goodison—they were responsible for his royal barge, which bears a very similar motif. A very ornate, tall oval mirror with pendulous flowers hanging from the base and surmounted with a bearded head with feathered crown—but the design has a simple unity.

Two Children by Sir G. Kneller, late seventeenth century (Dulwich Picture Gallery). Another beautifully carved frame with naturalistic leaves and flowers.

The Marquis de St Paul by Jean-Baptiste Greuze, c. 1760 (Rijksmuseum, Amsterdam). A very simple oval design for this frame (signed by A. Levert on the back) shows the reaction to the extravagance of rococo.

Chippendale mirror in Rowton Castle, Salop, UK. A plain oval frame, but with fanciful birds with stretched beaks and flapping wings, and with ornaments much more fanciful than those of Grinling Gibbons protruding from the outer edge.

The Prince of Wales, 1755 (Victoria and Albert Museum, London). Another frame of Chippendale's: an example of an English version of rococo.

Mrs Siddons by Thomas Gainsborough, c. 1758 (National Gallery, London). A 'Maratta' frame, derived from a late seventeenth-century Italian design by Carlo Maratta. This was very popular in England, even as late as the nineteenth century (at which time the ornament began to be made of plaster composition instead of being carved wood).

Portrait of a Lady, artist unknown, c. 1780 (Waddesdon Manor, Aylesbury). A classical oval frame crowned with a rather exuberant wreath of flowers with crossed branches. Signed by T. Dumont on the back.

Library, Kenwood (London). Robert Adam and his brother brought the classical revival to England, but their inspiration came from a visit to Italy rather than from French neo-classicism. The mirror over the mantelpiece has a typical example of an Adam frame.

Library at Osterley Park, 1766. Designed by Robert Adam. Framed painting by Antonio Zucchi over the mantelpiece shows how frame design had become subservient to the décor.

Harewood House, Yorkshire, UK. Chippendale and Robert Adam worked together on the interior decoration of this house. Adam's mirror frames of gilded wood are often oval, with projecting husks and hanging festoons upheld by cupids, surmounted by urns.

State bedroom, Harewood House, Yorkshire. The Adam mirror has a small round picture at the top of the frame and ornament of winged horses; the whole ornate structure almost touches the ceiling.

Pole-screen, third quarter of the eighteenth century (Victoria and Albert Museum: W.34–1959). Carved mahogany, delicate thin Georgian frame with a watercolour probably of a later date.

Col. George K. H. Coussmaker, Grenadier Guards, 1782 (Metropolitan Museum of Art, New York). An eighteenth-century British frame in classical Louis XVI style.

Portrait by Pierre-Paul Prud'hon (Rijksmuseum, Amsterdam). This pastel painting has a French Empire frame, with plaster ornament on concave moulding sharply delineated.

The Haywain by John Constable, 1821. The nineteenth-century framers imitated designs from the past, using moulded plaster composition for the ornament. This is in imitation of a French *Régence* pattern.

Seascape by Hendrik W. Mesdag, nineteenth century (Rijksmuseum, Amsterdam). Typically bright, ornate frame—designed with décor in mind rather than the picture itself.

Landscape by K. G. Bilders, nineteenth century (Rijksmuseum, Amsterdam). Copy of Louis XIII frame with a wide ornate floral pattern.

The Blessed Damozel by Dante Gabriel Rossetti, nineteenth century (Lever Collection, Port Sunlight, USA). The Pre-Raphaelite painters rebelled against the lack of aesthetic taste of their contemporaries and often designed their own highly original frames. This one has Gothic columns and a painted predella.

Beata Beatrix by Dante Gabriel Rossetti, 1872 (Art Institute of Chicago). Rossetti has added a painting on the predella of his frame showing the meeting of Dante and Beatrice in Paradise.

Old Battersea Bridge by James McNeill Whistler, nineteenth century (Tate Gallery, London). Whistler has made the delicate ornament on this frame of his slightly asymmetrical to harmonize with the composition of the picture.

Honfleur, Evening, Mouth of the Seine by Georges Seurat, 1886 (Museum of Modern Art, New York). One of Seurat's frames painted in the same pointillist manner as his pictures.

Le Crotoy, Looking Downstream by Georges Seurat, 1889 (Detroit Institute of Arts). The largest surviving frame of Seurat, it shows the lines of the sandbanks carried across the frame in brush-strokes of complementary colours.

Le Crotoy, Looking Upstream by Georges Seurat, 1889 (Stavros S. Niarchos Collection). Exhibited as a pair with above.

A Garden in Calmphout by Henry van de Valde, 1890 (Bavarian State Museum, Munich). Another artist who has made his frame painted in a pointillist technique, but with a reeded moulding.

Two Children Are Threatened by a Nightingale by Max Ernst, 1924 (Museum of Modern Art, New York). A surrealist's frame, using carved wooden objects.

La Représentation by René Magritte, 1937 (Penrose Collection, London). A fairly plain wide gilt frame moulded to the unusual shape of the picture.

Café Lipp, Paris, 1900 (photograph, Lucinda Lambton Library). Art nouveau tiling and plain dark wooden wall frames.

Daisy Fairy by Peter Blake, 1981–2 (Waddington Galleries, London). Carved frame in an asiatic style.

Eglentyne by Peter Blake, 1981–2 (Waddington Galleries, London). Very ornate gilt baroque frame, almost as wide as the picture.

The Owl and the Pussycat by Peter Blake, 1981–3 (Bristol Museum and Art Gallery). Embossed copper frame with sinuous flowers running up the sides and a setting sun on the sea with a boat. Blake has used the shape of this boat in the picture itself.

BIBLIOGRAPHY

Doerner, M., *The Materials of the Artist*, (Granada, 1979)

Heydenryk, H., *The Art and History of Frames*, (Nicholas Vane, 1964)

McNamara, D., *Picture Framing*, (David and Charles, 1986)

O'Neill, I., *The Art of the Painted Finish for Furniture and Decoration*, (Morrow Quill, 1971)

Osborne, H., Ed., *The Oxford Companion to the Decorative Arts*, (Oxford University Press, 1985)

Swarbrick, J., *Works in Architecture of R. and J. Adam*, (Tiranti, 1959)

INDEX